em three
"Fast, funky and original"
Tina Jackson
The Big Issue

PRETEXT

Volume 5 Spring 2002

Editors: Ali Smith & Julia Bell
Contributing Editor: Peter Bush
Copy-editing & Typesetting: Julian p Jackson
Proofreading: Peter Holm-Jensen
Subscriptions and Marketing: Simon Brett & Sara Wingate Gray
For subscriptions and advertising contact: info@penandinc.co.uk

Thanks to the following people for making this magazine possible: The Arts Council of England, the Regional Arts Lottery Programme, Jon Cook and Val Striker at UEA, Katri Skala, the Centre for Creative and Performing Arts, UEA, everyone at Signature, and all our contributors for allowing us to publish their work.

Pretext is a Pen&inc publication for EAS Publishing, 2002
Pen&inc, English and American Studies, University of East Anglia, Norwich, NR4 7TJ

ISBN: 1-902913-13-2

Pretext is published by Pen&inc at the University of East Anglia and distributed by Signature Books, Sunhouse, 2–4 Little Peter Street, Manchester, M15 4PS admin@signature-books.co.uk Tel: 0161 834 8767

Printed and bound by Biddles Ltd, Woodbridge Park, Guildford.

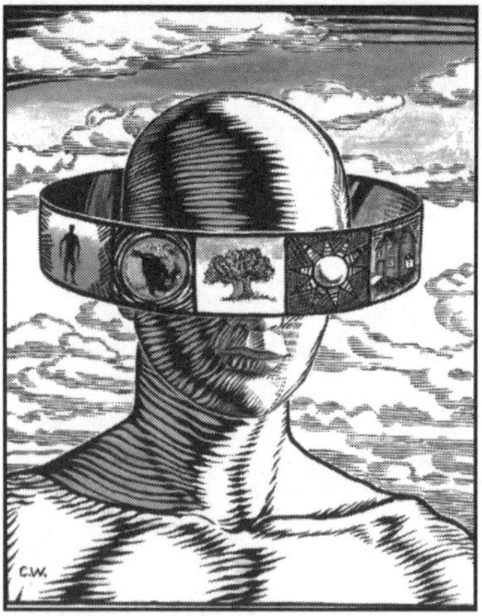
C.W.

The British Centre for Literary Translation

British Centre for Literary Translation

The 2002
St Jerome Lecture on Literary Translation

Susan Sontag

23 September 2002,
Queen Elizabeth Hall,
South Bank Centre,
London

An unmissable opportunity to hear one of America's leading writers and intellectuals

The evening also includes the presentation of the European Translation Prizes 2002.

Discover the latest in contemporary fiction from across Europe or take a new look at a much loved classic.

Join us for an evening celebrating literature in translation.

Details from:
British Centre for Literary Translation,
University of East Anglia,
Norwich NR4 7TJ
email bclt@uea.ac.uk

Contents

The Bodies Vest 1
Kate Atkinson

Poetry 13
Ramona Herdman

Perpetual Motion 17
Graeme Gibson

Three Stories 27
Helle Helle
***Translated by* Peter Holm-Jensen**

Why Don't You Stop Talking 31
Jackie Kay

Interview with Kathy Acker 41
Kasia Boddy

Stick Figures 59
Stella Duffy

Passage Migrants 67
D.J. Taylor

More Chips and Scraps 73
Rachel Bradford

Penny and Marilyn 77
Nell Dunn

Nothing is Serious 83
Sarah Wood

Taxonomy 101
Donald Paterson

A Story Out Of Sorts 111
Kasia Boddy

Pink and Blue 115
Frances Gapper

Red Roof 119
Louise Tondeur

Poetry 133
Egon Schiele
***Translated by* Will Stone & Anthony Vivis**

Airports Don't Count 143
Steve Chamberlain

Poetry 155
Graham Mort

The Meeting 159
Sidura Ludwig

Owl and Pussycat, Some Years Later 167
Margaret Atwood

Biographical Notes 173

‘There’s no way to categorize the writing.’
– Kathy Acker

In memory of Lorna Sage and W.G. Sebald

Kate Atkinson
THE BODIES VEST

Vincent's father, Billy, died a woman's death in 1959. He had been washing the windows of their tiny Glaswegian eyrie and in an act of reckless bravado tried (and fatally failed) to reach the awkward top corner of the living-room bay. Billy was just twenty-four years old, a reluctant widower who had embraced his role as Vincent's lone parent with enthusiastic incompetence. Vincent's mother, Georgie, was already four years dead by the time her foolish husband plummeted onto the cracked concrete path in front of their tenement home on one of the long summer evenings of Vincent's childhood.

Vincent had a good view of his father's final moments, sitting, as he was, one neighbouring storey lower, in the window of Mrs Anderson's flat, finishing off a supper of fried potatoes and Lorne sausage. Mrs Anderson was a homely barge of a woman, her grandmotherly bulk wrapped in a flowered Empire apron, who supplemented Vincent's rather meagre diet with a bottomless cornucopia of custard creams and bread and dripping. Mrs Anderson's small polished flat, scalloped everywhere with beige crochet mats and antimacassars and perfumed with Lifebuoy and fried mince, was a haven of domestic bliss compared to Vincent's own home. For all Billy's efforts at housekeeping, father and son occupied a dingy sett in which every available surface seemed to be crumbed with cigarette ash and desiccated fragments of pan loaf. Their clothes, washed to a uniform scummy grey, were hung to dry on the pulley above the gas cooker so that the scent of fried bacon was always on their skin.

Worst of all, perhaps, were the bed sheets, unwashed from one month to the next, pastel-striped flannelette on which no pastel stripes were now discernible and which were heavily impregnated with tangy male aromas. Vincent shared a bed with Billy even though there was a small box bed in the wall that would have done very well for him if it hadn't been occupied by an old dismembered BSA motorbike.

The windows, the cause of Vincent's orphan status at the tender age of six, had not been washed since his mother's funeral when Mrs Anderson had paid her own window cleaner to take care of them as a mark of respect. Vincent was two years old when Georgie died and had no memory of her at all so that what he felt was her absence rather than her loss. Vincent had an image of what life would have been like if his mother had lived. It involved living in a warm house and eating fruit and grilled chops, wearing clean, ironed pyjamas and sitting in front of a blazing coal fire while Georgie read out loud to him from *The Dandy*. Both Billy and Mrs Anderson implied, in their own ways, that it wouldn't necessarily be like that if Georgie was still around. 'Georgie was . . . flighty,' Mrs Anderson said, searching for an enigmatic word, so that Vincent imagined his mother as a ball of feathers wafted on a kindly wind.

Scant evidence remained of Billy and Georgie's existence as a couple, only a photograph on the sideboard in a tarnished frame which showed them on their wedding-day looking far too young to make solemn vows about anything, let alone the rest of their lives. Billy was eighteen, Georgie sixteen. 'Already up the duff,' Billy explained sadly to Vincent when they occasionally contemplated this photograph together. In her knee length, cheap bridal white, bird-boned Georgie looked as though she was attending her confirmation not her wedding, while Billy's jockey physique was ill fitted to his borrowed suit. Even their names hinted at a childishness they would never grow out of. When Vincent himself was grown-up, he wondered if this was why they had given their unlooked-for son such a mature name – although later still Vincent suspected that he might have been named for the Vincent Rapide motorbike. As with most things to do with Billy and Georgie, it was too late to ask. Vincent supposed he was lucky he hadn't been called 'Norton'.

Many years after their absurdly untimely deaths Billy came into possession of their wedding certificate but the 'William Stanley Petrie' and 'Georgina Rose Shaw' who were incorporated at Gretna Green in 1953 seemed to have little to do with the happy-go-luckily named Billy and Georgie of that nuptial photograph with their cheery smiles and accident-prone natures.

No one ever really discovered what happened to Georgie, of course. The way Billy told it she went out one evening and never came back – a simple narrative that explained nothing. Mrs Anderson's version of the tale was more complex – his mother had gone out for a drink with some friends, she was a 'very friendly' girl apparently, and had been found in a close the next morning by a milkman, strangled with one of her own stockings. 'No one deserved that,' Mrs Anderson sometimes said to Vincent, in a way that suggested his mother might have deserved other bad things that fell only slightly short of murder by persons unknown.

The last of the fried potatoes were cold and ketchup-sodden and Vincent's appetite had already moved on to a plate of snowballs sitting pristinely on Mrs Anderson's checked cloth when his father fell past the window like a wet sandbag. Billy's end had been presaged by the watery arc and clank of his galvanized bucket a split-second before Billy himself was pushed into space by the invisible hand of fate. Billy made no sound at all except for the muffled thud of his landing, a strangely anticlimactic noise like a shell failing to explode. Mrs Anderson, in a moment of elderly distraction muttered, 'There he goes again,' as if Billy annoyed her on a regular basis with his giddy antics. Vincent had expected to look out of the window and see Billy laughing and dusting himself off and was surprised when all he saw was a crumpled heap, not immediately recognizable as his father.

Like Georgie before him, Billy was cremated, leaving nothing for Vincent but a few atoms dancing on the air.

Someone, somehow, traced Georgie's parents, or 'Mr and Mrs Shaw', as they seemed to prefer to be called. (It was with some difficulty that Mrs Shaw finally settled on 'Grandmother' as an acceptable epithet.) Mr and Mrs Shaw ran a guest house in

Scarborough called (somewhat mendaciously) 'Sea-View'. They accepted Vincent into their lives with considerable reluctance. 'You were the last thing we were expecting,' Mrs Shaw said, as if Vincent was a disappointment rather than a surprise.

A small attic room was cleared for Vincent. Georgie's old room had already been turned into a guest bedroom after Mr and Mrs Shaw decided some time ago that Georgie wasn't coming home. They were right. The last her parents had seen of Georgie was when she left the house one evening to go to the pictures with a girlfriend and never came back. It seemed disappearing was more of a personality trait than a consequence for Vincent's mother, although of course it later emerged that she hadn't met the girlfriend nor gone to the pictures but had run off with a fairground worker, a weasel-faced Scottish youth who had spun her round on the Waltzer before leading her astray on the beach. 'A greasy gypsy' according to Mrs Shaw. It was some time before Vincent understood that she was talking about Billy, his father. Vincent didn't think that Billy was actually a gypsy, he may have led an itinerant life but he had looked and spoken like a badly nourished Glaswegian.

Mr and Mrs Shaw had never met Billy, of course, and in their version of Georgie's life he was a swarthy ogre of a man who had carried off their not very innocent child. Even her own parents had to admit that Georgie was a 'bit of a handful'. Nonetheless, Georgie had been in possession of a school certificate, good RSA speeds (junior secretary in the planning offices of Scarborough district council!) and had had a future ahead of her as the wife of some respectable East Coast burgher, instead of which she had debunked with a microscopic Vincent in her belly and fled to Gretna Green.

'She didn't have to do that,' Mrs Shaw told Vincent irritably, 'we would have stood by her. Someone would have adopted you.'

Mrs Shaw 'ran a tight ship' at the guest house and Mr Shaw, a man somewhat lacking in personality, remained firmly second-in-command to his wife, fetching and carrying breakfasts and coal scuttles and wholesale boxes of breakfast cereals. Mealtimes for guests were announced with a gong and were served with commendable precision by Mr Shaw and a squint-eyed girl called

Lorna who slipped Vincent forbidden chocolate digestives when Mrs Shaw wasn't looking. Vincent and Lorna ate together in the kitchen at odd hours in between the gong, dining on toast and marmalade – a more palatable meal they both agreed than the leftovers Mrs Shaw expected them to eat.

Sea-View was a veritable reliquary of Georgie's effects – a scratched and muddied hockey stick in the tool shed, her first pair of Start-Rite sandals in a sideboard drawer. Her autograph book ('Georgie Shaw's book – do not read on pain of death!') nestled amongst Mr Shaw's Flanders and Swann records and contained the mundane testimonials of her classmates ('Roses are red, violets are blue, sugar is sweet and so are you' being the favourite token of no less than four of her secondary school connoisseurs). Vincent was particularly intrigued by the countless well-kept albums of photographs, which charted Georgie's progress from premature birth but which stopped slightly short of her premature death.

Many of Georgie's girlish possessions had been boxed up and placed in the cellar where sea-air and mildew had wreaked havoc on them. Her jewellery case, a musical box with a pert ballerina on the top, had rusted so much that the dancer now executed her pirouettes with an odd jerky intensity to the discordant music of metal grating on metal. Vincent was sad that he would never know what tune had once played on the box. ('*Clair de la lune?*' Mr Shaw hazarded with little conviction). Georgie's books – stories of wholesome, enterprising boarding-school girls with bemusing names like Jinty and Jax and Pippa – had become foxed and limp and smelt of earth.

Her collection of expensive dolls – sitting now on an ottoman in the Shaws' bedroom – had weathered better. Pale-faced and rosebud-lipped, they wore inscrutable expressions as they waited stoically for their owner to return. Vincent was forbidden to play with the dolls as the Shaws had developed a fear that his puny body and pale adenoidal countenance put him at risk of turning into 'a fairy' – a fate that sounded infinitely more attractive to Vincent than one where he was harried and bullied at school and largely overlooked at home, especially after Lorna left abruptly one morning after being discovered by Mrs Shaw in one of the guest bedrooms doing something unspeakable with Mr Shaw. Mr Shaw was allowed to stay on but from then on was treated by Mrs Shaw as little more than a deckhand.

From his attic perch, Vincent observed the family life he had always been denied – guests coming and going with their burdens of rubber buckets and spades, fishing nets and beach balls. The fighting, pinching, squealing children, the fretful mothers, the holidaying paterfamiliases attempting to sustain bonhomie – it all looked as mysterious as the adventures of Jinty. The Shaws never took Vincent to the beach, a place they held in contempt, and he was almost a teenager before it struck him that he could go there any time he wanted, although he hardly ever did as the Front was too disturbing – full of noise and sweat and stickiness. Vincent did not like the sea, he did not see a limitless grey horizon, he saw a careless edge over which anyone might fall and vanish into an infinite limbo.

Vincent's little bedroom was four storeys up so that he was able to get a good idea of how far Billy himself had fallen on his final day. Sometimes Vincent viewed it from the other way round – standing on the pavement looking up and trying to imagine what the expression on his father's face must have been when he found himself plunging to earth like a suddenly flightless bird. Vincent supposed it was one of astonishment.

Vincent had formed a theory – at the moment of death, he believed, a person would be doing the very thing that would have made him happiest in life. He hadn't known Billy well enough to be sure what that might have been but decided, in the absence of proof otherwise, that Billy flew off to his end on the seat of a 1952 Royal Enfield Bullet, a smile of bliss transforming his peaky face.

The Shaws liked Vincent best when he was quiet, so he spent the rest of his childhood keeping out of the way. He became a bookish boy, introverted and obsessive, yet slightly more sanguine than might have been expected. When he was eventually accepted into a more than half-decent university to read English, Mrs Shaw remarked – by way of congratulation – that he must have got his brains from his mother, because he certainly hadn't got them from his father.

Mr and Mrs Shaw died in their separate beds many years later and long after Sea-View and its contents had gone up in flames while they were away visiting Mrs Shaw's sister in Warrington. When Vincent received the news of the fire he thought sadly of Georgie's dolls, their nylon hair incandescent, their patient plastic faces melting like candle wax. He thought, too, of Jinty and Jax and Pippa, once game for anything and now reduced to papery ash. Most of all he felt for the pert ballerina, her tiny foot stilled forever, mid-pirouette. There was not even one photograph of Georgie left now; Vincent's mother had been successfully erased from history. Vincent did not dwell on this tragedy, however, because at the time that the last earthly relics of Georgie were being carbonized he was having round-the-clock sex with Nanci Zane and fearing that his brain might actually explode with ecstasy.

Vincent met Nanci Zane on a passenger ferry bound for Naxos when she came to his aid during a panic attack ('Hi, I'm Nanci with an '*i*' – breathe into this paper bag.') Nanci-with-an-i diagnosed agoraphobia caused by being afloat on so much sea. This was 1977 and Nanci was on a world tour after college ('Berkeley – English major') travelling alone except for a huge rucksack which Vincent could barely lift. Nanci thought Vincent was cute. She mistook his timidity for reserve, his neuroses for eccentricity, his self-deprecating irony for sparkling wit – in short, he was the perfect English gentleman, particularly if you were an orthodontist's daughter from Sacramento who had never met an English gentleman before, perfect or otherwise.

Vincent was bewitched by Nanci's foreignness. For starters, she had a name beginning with a 'Z' (or a 'Zee' in Nanci's xenurine alphabet) and was almost unnaturally healthy - not only a vegetarian but a devotee of almost every form of exercise that Vincent had heard of and several he had not – the first person he'd ever met who did 'aerobics', something which at first Vincent thought had to do with airborne germs. She was also the first person Vincent had ever encountered with perfect teeth, teeth which 'Dad' had devoted much of his spare time to and which were indeed pearly – something Vincent had presumed was a figure of speech until he saw Nanci's small, opalescent molars and incisors. Her skin seemed to have been buffed and polished and it retained its California blush, even beneath the alien Manchester skies to which he subjected her while he finished his doctoral thesis – 'Body and Soul: the transcendence of death in Metaphysical Poetry.' ('Wow,' Nanci said, 'sounds cool.') Nanci 'wrote a little poetry' too but it tended towards Hallmark rather than Plath. Vincent told her it showed fantastic promise.

Nanci 're-rowted' her world tour after Naxos and went back to England with Vincent, sharing the poky redbrick terrace he rented, her wanderlust temporarily on hold while she took a course in art history and cooked complex complementary protein meals from the *Moosewood Cookbook* before demanding energetic sex. Sex with Nanci had a sporty rather than an erotic feel to it and after particularly vigorous sessions she would collapse (for a few seconds at any rate) and say, 'Wow, what a fantastic workout, Vince,' so that Vincent experienced pride for the first time in his life. Once, he asked her what the answer was that she'd worked out but she didn't understand his feeble joke.

For no obvious reason that Vincent could discern, Nanci suggested they get married. Which they did with absolutely no fuss in a registrar office. Nanci wore a dirndl skirt, a denim shirt and a crocheted waistcoat and braided her brown hair in two thick Saxon plaits. For her bouquet, she carried a bunch of daffodils and was congratulated by a horde of friends all of whom she had accumulated with consummate ease in six months of living in Manchester. Nanci herself was the only friend of Vincent's at the wedding.

Vincent had absolutely no idea what Nanci saw in him but presuming it must be something to do with his Englishness he tried to play to his strengths – buying tweedy jackets with elbow patches, wearing spectacles he didn't really need and riding an old 1950s bicycle to and from university where he was now a junior lecturer.

Vincent and his new bride planned to abandon their damp Lancastrian abode at the end of the academic year and take a trip to California from which Vincent hoped very much that they wouldn't return. Nanci's family couldn't wait to meet Vincent apparently. The orthodontist had five daughters who all, from photographic evidence, looked just like Nanci, who was the youngest. Vincent thought of them as 'the Zane Sisters,' like quintuplets or a singing troupe. The whole family, even a couple of aunts, wrote letters to Vincent, welcoming him into their 'tribe'. Nanci's mother signed herself 'Mom'. Vincent couldn't wait to be absorbed into their miraculous, mysterious midst. He wondered if he could change his name to theirs – 'Vince Zane' sounded so much more interesting (a cowboy or a gangster perhaps) than Vincent Petrie. His surname was the only thing that remained of his father now. 'And you,' Nanci said, 'you're his legacy, too, honey.'

Nanci had a rogue wisdom tooth which was the subject of endless professional sounding conversations on the phone with her father in California, during which they debated whether or not she should wait for him to fix it or put herself in the hands of a dentist to whom she was a stranger. Nanci was the favourite child of 'Dad' and consulted him about most things, tooth-related or not. In the end, the tooth became so painful that Nanci opted to have it done by an NHS dentist. Her father recommended full anaesthesia although the NHS dentist took some persuading, accustomed as he was to inflicting pain.

Vincent was giving a tutorial when the police arrived, a male and a female constable, who hovered politely on the threshold of the room as if they couldn't bring themselves to interrupt his ramblings on Henry Vaughan. They came with supportive expressions already fixed on their faces. Vincent had a surge of guilt at the sight of them although the last illegal thing he had done was to try – and fail – to smoke a joint in 1973.

They explained everything very carefully to him in the car on the way to the hospital but try as he might Vincent couldn't understand what they were saying. Even in the mortuary where he identified Nanci's body he still couldn't understand why she lay insensible and waxy with a large hospital sheet pulled up to her chin, 'Just like a corpse,' he said to the policewoman, who frowned and stared at the floor. Vincent was expecting Nanci to fling the sheet off and jump off the hospital trolley.

But she didn't because she'd had a massive reaction to the

anaesthetic in the dentist's chair and her heart had stopped and could not be persuaded to start again.

Nanci's family asked Vincent if he would mind if her body was shipped back to Sacramento and, seeing as there were so many more of them than there was of him, he felt it would have been churlish to refuse. The day Nanci was flown away in the cargo hold of an America-bound Boeing he spent his last minutes with her alone in the Co-operative Funeral Home. He had considered snipping off one of her plaits as a keepsake, the bright hair about the bone and so on, but in the end had decided it might look to obvious and anyway he wanted something more essential, something coralline or chalky – the bedrock of Nanci-with-an-i. To this end he came armed with bolt-cutters, purchased as furtively as a murder weapon from a local ironmonger. 'Sorry about this,' Vincent whispered to a silently decaying Nanci as he snipped off her little finger, wrapped it in a paper napkin and slipped it in his pocket.

As he stood on the observation deck at Manchester airport and silently saluted his cold, slightly incomplete, wife, as she rose into the sky he clutched her finger in his hand. It wasn't the whole Nanci. But it was something. He hoped that at the moment of death she had found herself in the middle of a truly great workout and that it had given her the answers to all the questions she hadn't had time to ask.

'A relative?' a woman on the observation desk asked him as he gazed like an augur at the skies.

'My wife,' Vincent affirmed.

'She'll be back soon,' the woman said, sensing the quiver in Vincent's voice.

Vincent doubted that very much but he didn't say so.

If the Zanes noticed that a bit of Nanci was missing they never said so. They kept in touch with Vincent over the years. The sisters sent him photographs of weddings and christenings and family celebrations. He garnered formal portraits of various combinations of Zanes as well as less formal snaps of younger Zanes – in Little League livery, in Halloween rig, in gowns and mortar boards. They all looked alike and Vincent had no idea who any of them were. 'Mom' sent him Christmas cards although a couple of years down the line she changed into 'Ellen' as if she had realized how absurd it was to call herself mother to a man she had never met. 'Dad' never wrote because he killed himself with a shotgun right after Nanci's death.

Vincent had thought about killing himself too but he was in thrall to such a numbing inertia that he found it difficult to do anything so decisive. For months afterwards he slept with the finger beneath his pillow and tried to dream about Nanci, but she never came. At first he had allowed the finger to mummify on the mantelpiece but it had arrived at such a disagreeable state, hard and wrinkled and so unlike Nanci's living digit, that he had rendered it – stewing it for hours in an old aluminium saucepan. This was not an act undertaken lightly and Vincent retched violently several times during the course of his unholy cuisine. He was satisfied with the result he achieved, however – the clean, white bone that was freighted with a kind of magic. Of lesser things have saints been made, Vincent thought.

Vincent carried the finger bone in his pocket as other men might have carried a lucky coin or talismanic charm. Vincent hoped that if there was a Judgement Day – something he thought unlikely in the extreme – that on the world's last night Nanci's soul wouldn't come looking for her body and discover it needed her stolen finger in order to be fully resurrected.

When Vincent himself died, the finger bone was found and discarded by his wife as part of the meaningless jetsam of her husband's life.

Vincent died too young, everyone agreed, but in the end it was a peaceful 'crossing over' (his wife's preferred term.) A virulent cancer had started in his lymph nodes and quickly metastasized first into his liver and then into his bones. At the end he was wreathed in morphine but right up until the last day was still able to recognize his wife and sons – two headstrong, angry teenagers quite cowed by his illness. He wanted to tell them that everything was all right, but he couldn't speak and besides he had no logical evidence on which to base that belief.

When Vincent entered into the world of light he was in the company of Georgie, exquisitely real and vivid in a way she never had been for him before. He was holding her hand and they were watching a flock of birds that were flying overhead. Starlings, Vincent noted, a species of bird he hadn't previously realised he liked so much.

Georgie herself, since you ask, was spinning round on the Waltzer when her soul took flight, forever sixteen and all her life ahead of her.

Ramona Herdman
POETRY

'Ours is a mighty God'

I sang it, on the platform that you stood me on,
as bridesmaid, love.
I sang your lies; I would have praised your cat,
for the honour you'd done me. You were as maid
as white deserved. I hope the wedded night was good.
And that you kept that other good that holds you up.
I hope you held yourself virtuous still, past the line that ruled
this justified. Myself, I can't love anything I can't hold in one hand.
My hamster does. I can cram all it wants in a chocolate drop.
My friend, your face in a veil I can love –
there by the vicar and the groom and the microphone stand
it is as small as the ring I hand you. I can love you,
since I only understand you in two terms – the love
with which you say 'all that I am' to your groom
and the love for your odd idea of a God –
big as the necessary explosion of this room.

Cat learns to frown

She doesn't like her kittens.
She doesn't like the pull,
the release through the teats,
the way you're supposed to feel.

It's as if her feet have fallen off
and have to be watched forever.
As if a bit could get run over by itself –
the memory of a stoned riverbank summer

or how to whistle – lost.
She's made something now,
something like a sieve to sail.
Her guts around her feet making a row

with their small impossible mouths.
They're the birds come back to haunt her.
She doesn't like their wet-feather tails
and how they have to want her.

Ramona Herdman

Buzz

Sugar flings wasps into the lower branches of psychosis
like someone else's bright red shoes,
tight-laced for kisses.

The digging in, the dogwood welts
against the bliss of snow-bright biting skies.
They tap themselves out, fleeing steel-soled,
stiletto legs a danger to themselves,
an awkward black-gold threat.

Wasps are zipped from talon tip to
tongue to hypodermic to bondage stripes
to tail tip in speed and coke and fear.
It's a constant head-rush windowpane
flying fuck in plastic nails.

All for the soft and damned release –
the morphine of the jam jar,
the wet dream of an opium den.

We make eternity rings of them
or snap them at the corset point.
Wasps rot to the quick –
two linked black teeth,
fizzing and soaring with want.

Fat women that panted and thin women that burned, old women that dreamed

– Raymond Chandler, *Farewell my Lovely*

Nights I'm the only one here I get dim and lonesome,
dull and lowdown. I dye my hair. I change the sheets.
I lie there and think what they're missing.
Perfume behind the soft underfold of ear.
The bombs outside would be further, the blue murder
off in a blue moon if he were here.

If he were here, so what? The bed would be overhot,
undersized. Another pair of eyes does not
do away with the desert. They never adore
the right bits. Sometimes I wish I could gingham and brisk
away all the lip gloss and tits, the years
and the polish, the murmurs and spit.

Last night I dreamt of ants – there wasn't a tree left
in all the treed canyon for mine to nest
and bristle in. I've never felt
so much a lion and I've woken all tooth and maw.
I'm not waiting any longer. It's not twilight anymore.
I'm off to dance with the bombs – it's what the burning in me's for.

Graeme Gibson
Perpetual Motion

'. . . and let me not be ashamed of my hope.'
– Psalm 119

With the rushing of wings, darkness gathered in the forest behind him. Robert Fraser stretched, rubbed his head with both hands, and cautiously arched his back to ease the pain.

Late that morning when his ploughshare had caught and held fast, he'd cursed the bloody rocks, the tree stumps, the roots and the land. Ned and Smoke had paused, and then soothed by his voice leaned back into their harness with the uncertain excitement of animals remembering previous defeats. He'd strained against the handles, coaxing, driving with his legs and bearing down until he felt the obstruction lifting. He watched incredulously as it broke the surface, an enormous yellow bone rising to meet him. It was as long and thicker than his leg and for an instant he heard it like breath escaping the body. 'Whoa,' he shouted at the horses, recoiling as the bone shuddered against the mouldboard. Smoke was trembling, prancing as if the earth had begun to scorch her feet. Even Ned was agitated. Feeding them strands of tobacco, massaging and pulling their ears, he whispered a confidence he scarcely felt.

After scraping mud in strips from along its length, crouching beside it at last, he cleaned both ends. He worked methodically. Poking at it with his belt knife, he decided it was the leg bone of an elephant, it had to be! He knew about elephants, astonishing creatures with small dark men riding on their heads. Once in

Toronto he'd discovered that an elephant had left the previous day for Montreal. After dinner the men had recounted how a handsome young woman in costume had permitted herself to be encircled by the animal's sinuous trunk and then, to the astonishment of the crowd, she'd been lifted high in the air where she gracefully waved her arms and arched her back. Patting his waistcoat smooth with both hands, one had described how the young woman, now supine upon a Moorish carpet, had commanded the beast to rest its foot directly on her face. Nobody had ever seen anything like it and from time to time she comes to Fraser in dreams, a slim and pretty woman, neat in her brilliant costume, a simple tension in her arching back and loins – she postures elegantly, her arms beating the air like wings.

His pipe lit, he'd contemplated the bone for the better part of half an hour, in a welcome drying wind that burst from the treetops, gathered momentum across his field and whipped the smoke away from his mouth almost before he exhaled. With strands of dirty hair slapping his forehead and cheek, his trousers trembling the length of his calves, he crouched in concentration, his body folded down upon a rock. The bone rested across three furrows, with the shadows of clouds rushing on the land. He didn't see the straggle of wild pigeons shoot low over his field, nor hear the querulous shriek of a hawk somewhere in the forest beyond his fence. Fearing an evil omen, as if with spring the earth had cast up a warning. he tried to understand if he should bury it again . . .

Lifting the bone impulsively, cradling it like an infant or a corpse, he heard it again: a telluric sigh, an infinitely resigned and mournful breath that resisted him as he straightened, weighed him down as he struggled onto the unworked ground at the edge of the bush. Releasing the bone, stepping back as it fell, he waited; nothing more happened. Fetching his shovel he drove it into the earth, to uncover another bone almost immediately. And then a third. One after the other he placed them on the ground by the first, meticulously reconstructing what he'd begun to disinter.

And so the day had progressed with the growing certainty an elephant could not have come to die here beneath his land. The bones he found were too old, too porous; he could have crushed the smaller vertebrae in his hands. Whatever the beast, it had been waiting long before that day six years earlier when Joshua Willow, the half-breed, had stopped and said, 'She starts here and runs to the stream.' Robert Fraser would never forget that moment. just twenty-four years old, he'd stood on his land for the first time, and it had been indistinguishable from everything else on the route. The monotony of the bush was overwhelming; it more than diminished, it threatened to absorb him, transform him into a thing, an object like the birds. He'd left Mad River with Joshua just after dawn and for five hours they had walked in the silence of a heart beating without movement or sound: each tree and tangle of bush was like the next, each turn in the path endlessly repeated what he had just seen; it was as if a dark cloth was being dragged across his eyes. Vegetation caught at his clothes, brushed his hands and face as if to hold him, to enclose him with tendrils and take root. While air had moved in sunlight among the treetops, the forest floor was damp and still.

Flat-faced and, silent, almost disapproving, Joshua Willow had watched Fraser stand appaled, barely able to hear the water he could not see; and somewhere to the north and west, less than a hundred paces from them, this intricate and marvellous cage of bones had been lying even then just below the surface of a small clearing in the forest.

With the rushing of wings, darkness gathered in the forest behind him. The wind subsided, leaving the earth unnaturally still. The noise of his breath, the fatigue of the body inside his clothes, the sudden rasp of his shovel against another immense bone – these now familiar sounds thundered in his ears like blood. High above him, torn and ragged clouds streamed northward as he dropped once more to his knees on the wet earth. Clearing carefully with his hands and belt knife, following the hard plunging curve of bone, he encountered a ridge that must have been the brow and then the first of two gaping sockets; both of them, indeed the entire skull, were clogged with dirt. After excavating the interior, he rolled it out of the shallow pit and manoeuvred it into place among the disinterred and reconstructed maze of bones spread out on the tangle of last year's growth.

Another clutch of pigeons circled rapidly over the forest, to alight in some beech trees at the other end of his fence. This time he heard the urgent wings and as he turned to watch them land he saw a larger flock away to the south. The birds in the wood had begun to call plaintively; half a dozen flew down to perch on the fence, their voices trilling, echoing curiously in his head.

With the distant sound of a gun from Casey's, he returned to the pit. Dragging an ochre tusk to the skull, he imagined a great beast moving irresistibly, bulling its way in the forest, the angular ribs, each separate vertebra in a line, the empty sockets, those grinding teeth bigger than his fist, all of it clothed again, rising on massive legs . . .

Finally, climbing to sit on his fence, filling his pipe and immensely weary, feeling the silent flight of bats about his head, he faced the grotesque jumble of yellowed bones. Light convulsed beyond the forest; yellow and orange it swelled to a sombre green, a shaft stabbed brightly up, throwing the tops of trees into relief before vanishing like lightning. Pausing to relight his pipe he heard the winnowing of wings falling above him; and the night wind, setting leaves in random motion, breathed on his face. Reaching for the ground with his foot, gingerly climbing down, pressing both hands into the small of his back, carefully he twisted and stretched, chewing the stem of his pipe until his muscles relaxed, the pain subsided.

'That's it,' he said. 'By Jesus, it can be done. I'll do it!'

Just before noon Annie Birdwood arrived with Joshua to preside at Mary Fraser's childbed. Uncommonly pale, she greeted Robert with a thin smile, an imperceptible squeeze of her hand. 'She's not begun yet, has she?' He shook his head. 'Relax then,' suddenly laughing. 'She will soon enough.'

A gust of wind moved in the forest as Joshua Willow, gesturing with the hook where his left hand should have been, went to shoot pigeons as if that was his only business. And now the wind shivered young fruit trees and set Robert's wind machines clattering in the yard. Atop a pole by the gate, flapping its wooden wings, a rooster with blue eyes bounced mechanically; while on another, a team of white-washed horses trod without progress, the stridulate wheels of their wagon turning in the air. The models rose and fell; driven by whirring cedar blades they squeaked and clacked, idiotically repeating each gesture as Mary appeared, her belly filling the door. Hens pecked with worn beaks, tapping wood on wood; sows jerked spasmodically from side to side; a donkey (the size of a small dog) dropped its head and kicked repeatedly with hinged legs; and farther from the house a lean creature, it struggled erect, the lower jaw flipped open and a whistling shriek issued from the faded mouth . . .

Mary's labour began during dinner as if she'd been waiting for her mother. The child gave a cry inside her, a muffled declaration that straightened her in her chair, forcing sweat to her forehead and under her pale eyes. While Annie Birdwood hustled her upstairs, he tried to recall if she'd been different that morning but couldn't remember. As her belly had grown over the months, so had his confusion; he'd watched the skin stretching like an animal's in bloat, like hide drying on a drum, and felt the body convulsing within her body, tentatively at first, then violently so that lumps shifted beneath the skin's violet surface, and he stopped looking at her. He knew how it was done with animals; he'd presided at the birth of pigs. Customarily he tied ropes to the protruding feet of calves and pulled them out; he'd reached up into heifers to seize a slippery foot. Is that what midwives did? He couldn't imagine how it was with women. Cows at a difficult birth lie panting, dumb, their swollen bellies heaving; they grunt in pain and sometimes bellow, their tongues lolling over yellow teeth.

He was splitting wood for the stove when Annie came to him and said, as he knew she would, 'I read the waters.' A vein pulsed at her temple and the planes of her skull shone beneath her face. 'And they speak of trouble.' He sank his axe into the chopping block and turned to her, resigned. She had dashed spring water into the cracked basin so it swirled against the clock, and she stared for signs, for portents, only she could see. 'Not right away. She'll be all right, so she will. The baby too. But later . . .' Along the road Dr Tom Sanderson appeared, a small dark figure on a swayback horse, followed by the Caseys on foot. 'They speak of trouble.'

'How so?' Shooting by the beaver meadow, Joshua was moving closer to the bones. His hook looped to the barrel with a rawhide thong; he'd scarcely miss a bird.

'Never you mind.' Annie's fingers fluttered gently on the back of Robert's hand. 'We're best not knowing these things.'

'Good day to you both,' cried the doctor, still at a distance, his voice reedy, slightly mocking in tone.

'But, Jesus Christ . . .' Robert's voice overlapped. Why have you told me then? Her eyes like egg whites. Why have you told me? She tried to squeeze his hands. It's God's will, she seemed to be saying, be brave, be brave . . . He wrenched free, turning to greet the others, but Annie spoke first.

'You'll not be needed here, Tom Sanderson. So don't think that you are. And you, Robert, bring a load of that wood. We'll be wanting it before morning.' Bustling among wind machines that were momentarily still, she called back over her shoulder, 'Come along, Missus Casey, we've work to do . . .'

Drifting like tall ships, thunderclouds gathered in the west. A flock of pigeons darted erratically behind the barn as Barbara Casey, quick as a hen, scurried into the house.

'Well, at least you'll offer us a drink, Robert Fraser, eh? Hah! It's your estate after all.' Sliding from the horse, Dr Tom dug enthusiastically at his crotch. 'Christ, she's bony.' Laughing shrilly like a child he added, 'Stella. Here, the nag . . . I didn't mean, oh no sir, not the old woman, you wouldn't catch me riding . . . Eh?' He winked and spat. '"You won't be needed here, Tom Sanderson!" I'll tell you boys . . .'

'That Joshua I heard shooting?' Strong as an ox, and often angry, Will Casey had the voice of a boy.

'He's a devil with a gun all right.' Still rummaging in the crotch of his voluminous trousers, Sanderson showed his yellow teeth. 'Myself, as you know . . . I couldn't hit a barn if I was inside it.' He grinned fiercely, knowing some believed he'd murdered the corporal, dropping him with a single shot to the back of his head.

Light was fading rapidly, the wind gusting as the storm approached; colours draining out of objects left them flat among pullulating shadows. The men settled themselves by the barn, listening to the clatter of the machines and thunder, full-throated, menacing beyond the enclosing walls of the forest.

'More often than not, a good storm like this'll bring them on.' Nodding to the doctor's words, Casey raised the bottle and drank; his armpit and the side of his shirt were black with sweat.

'That's true enough with cattle beasts,' he said, putting the bottle in Dr Tom's outstretched hand.

'You mark my words . . .' The doctor filled his mouth and swallowed quickly. 'It won't be long now!'

Robert sat with his hands between his knees on an upturned log facing the house. Pairs of swallows clung to the dead branches of trees lining the stream. Chittering crazily, they launched themselves in wild circles against the sky, hurtled low over the barnyard where animals stamped their feet waiting for the storm to break, waiting as Smoke cantered erratically along the fenceline, her breath in low impatient whinnies.

Robert's pipe was out; he tapped it against his boot, blew to clear the stem and casually remarked, 'She read the waters, Will. She said they spoke of trouble.'

'Well, Jesus, Robbie, she's been wrong before.' Crushing one square hand in the other, Casey cracked and pulled each knuckle vigorously, then reversed his grip and began again. 'Plenty of times,' he whispered. 'Plenty times she's wrong.' There were only eight or ten heartbeats now between the lightning and its thunder.

Springing suddenly to his feet, the doctor skipped and hopped like a marionette, his oversize suit flapping and cracking as if at some point he'd shrunk inside it. 'By Christ,' he cried, 'it's a terrible thing she does! And her own daughter, too, this time.' He had to raise his voice, shout above the gathering din. 'None of us know what fate we're born to. Good fortune or ill, they come and go as the Lord decides.'

Drops of rain the size of a child's fist were exploding in the dust by the time they reached the porch. Heaving in subsiding light, the forest abandoned itself to the storm as they sheltered by the log wall. They smelled the lightning before it shattered, and even with hands over their ears they heard it like boiling fat hitting a stove.

Shaken by the full diapason of rain and thunder, the house shuddered as they entered; it creaked and twisted in every mortice and joint. Except for the staccato brilliance of lightning, there was neither light nor darkness but gradations of shadow, a penumbral gloom in which two lamps had been lit, one by the stove, another on the long table: two brown pools that trembled violently until Robert closed the door.

On the table between Joshua and Barbara Casey, half submerged in their own shadows, lay two enormous grinding teeth. Fraser knew what they were. Oh, Jesus! He leaned against the log wall and closed his eyes.

'What have we got here?' Rubbing his hands briskly, Dr Tom approached the table with Casey at his heels.

'Teeth.' Robert cleared his throat and said again, 'teeth.'

'Teeth, for Chrissakes . . .' He reached past Joshua and cautiously touched one with his index finger. 'What sort of bloody tooth is that, eh?' As he bent closer to the lamp, his sharp features appeared to soften, his lips and protuberant eyes glistened like oil. 'Crikey!'

'Joshua found them.' Pausing, Barbara appealed to Fraser. 'Robert, he says there's the skeleton of some monster out there.'

'Not too long since she's been dug out either.' With flat cheekbones and hair the colour of gun metal, Joshua watched Fraser curiously, then reached to pick at the largest, rocking it with the hook. 'Must of been some big animal ' 'he said, 'eh?'

Robert pushed himself from the wall, shrugged and put a fresh bottle among them on the table, then went to wash his hands.

'Monster,' gargled Casey. 'Skeleton of what monster?'

Mimicked by broken shadows, Robert splashed water into the basin and rolled up his sleeves. 'How's Mary?'

'She's resting fine,' replied Annie from the bottom of the stairs. 'She'll be a while yet but she's fine.' Her grey hair undone was surprisingly full, a wiry bush shrouding her face and shoulders. 'Well, Robert,' she said, bringing cups from the shelf, 'what was it you found out there?'

'Yes, tell us, man.' The doctor was pouring whiskey even before she'd finished arranging the cups. 'What kind of an animal has teeth like that?'

'That's a tooth all right.' Casey had finally picked one up. 'Holy Mother of God.'

'No popery.' Annie didn't smile. 'What was it, Robert?'

'I don't know!' He pulled a stool into their circle. 'I haven't the faintest notion but I'll tell you I've never seen anything to match it alive or dead, and I've never heard tell of it either.'

Clustering in lamplight they took turns with the teeth; hefting intently, they pursed their lips, nodding as if they perceived the magic planes and shadows, the revealing weight within them. They listened gravely as Robert tried to find the words, some combination of words; but like an inarticulate Adam he found nothing to interpret or contain the mystery, and so he talked of his own wonder and confusion, the dumb conviction he should have reburied the first one, left well enough alone, and that terrible breath, dear God, as he'd clasped it against his body. He lifted his hands, reaching towards his breast; and afterwards they swore they'd heard it too, each of them, and as the days passed, the weeks and months, they became more certain: it was like a body's final breath, so it was, as if you'd thrown your weight on the chest of a corpse, or the sigh of a sleeper entering some dolorous territory of dream . . .

Angus was born after midnight with the guts of the storm well off to the south. Rain was falling steadily; rushing from eavestroughs it overflowed the rain barrels as the men heard a new sound in Mary's labour. Then Robert heard a small voice, a feral cry; it pierced his ears like needles.

When he could wait no longer, he climbed the stairs in his stocking feet. Stooping to peer into the room as if he'd become a stranger, with shadows massed on the side of his face like a birth scar, he had to resist the urge to creep back down to the others waiting by the fire, another bottle between them on the table.

Three women in candlelight at the head of his bed. Annie's high voice in a private song. She stood with her back to him, her head bowed, holding the child against her thin bosom while Barbara Casey helped Mary into the freshly made bed. The rain had passed but water fell crazily onto the roof from leaves and branches. He should have waited to be called.

Had a child really uttered that desolate cry, like something caught in the forest at night?

He spied on the women in the circle of light. Mary's legs, plump scissors, disappeared beneath the covers, the glowing flesh of arms and shoulders as Barbara Casey began to brush out her hair. Holding it from the head with her left hand, she pulled the brush sleepily from the scalp, then back again to the rhythm of

Annie's crooning chant. Her lovely hair, it crackled and shone about her face, so distant and serene he had to rest his forehead and cheek against the doorjamb.

'It's a boy.' Annie's face was empty, her body calm as she held the child up to him, an offering she didn't expect him to take. A small pinched face beneath a cap of damp fur; it wasn't much bigger than a potato. He didn't know what to say. Black hair curled tightly against the scalp like moss; the closed eyes were enormous and set to the side of its head like a fawn's.

The baby shuddered as he leaned to touch the tiny cheek, the jawline exquisite as a fishbone beneath his finger. Heavy drops of water splattered on the roof, a lone frog called from beside the pond as the mouth twisted; trying to catch his finger it opened to suck, a flash of teeth, a mewling cry struggled in its throat as he jerked his hand away.

'Are they supposed to have teeth?' He hadn't meant to say that. It didn't even sound like his voice. He shifted from one foot to the other and cleared his throat.

Robert was never to mention the teeth again. Because they slipped out of the baby's gums within the week, and Mary found most of them in his cradle, smooth and unblemished, with no roots at all, Robert was able to convince himself he'd been mistaken, they'd never been there; it was a story told by old women recalling dead babies or childbed fever.

'You'd best go now.' Mary lay with fingers curled on her flat belly, her eyes closed. 'You can tell the others you have a son.'

The baby convulsed in Annie's arms and gave a piercing cry before she could speak again. The face was brown and wrinkled as old fruit, the teeth like needles, rat's teeth, and as he fled the room he saw black hair like fur across the shoulders, it clustered down the spine. He saw Mary's face. Two women crouching over the bed, that urgent body wriggling like a ferret beneath their hands.

Helle Helle
Three Stories

From: Biler og dyr (Cars and Animals),
Samleren, 2000.
Translated by Peter Holm-Jensen

Eulogy

It was a dream that came back to me night after night, a classic, a typical dream: I suddenly discovered that the house I lived in contained an extra room. A big room in the attic, say, or in the basement, or behind the kitchen. I walked through the house and discovered it by accident. I was very happy. I wanted to furnish the room with chairs and tables and beds. So there was enough room where I lived after all. I could have guests staying overnight. Or I could turn it into an office. The house would now have risen in value, and the bank would probably lend me more money.

I woke up with backache. Unlike in the dream, I was not alone. I had a family: a husband and two children and a third on the way. I rolled onto the floor, lay there a little, then got up and had a bath. I could barely fit in the tub.

At breakfast I sat on two chairs. The children laughed. The coffee was strong and bitter. I thought of it as my only poisonous habit.

But then there was the doorway, which I stood in, big and threatening: You're not listening to me! We don't have enough space! I pointed at my stomach: It would get worse and worse. Then you got up from the table and went out and put your coat on, and the children followed you. You're not listening to me! You never listen to what I say!

How often did I not sit and fantasize when you had all gone. I could sit like that for hours, with my eyes closed to avoid the sight of all the mess.

I apologize. I take it all back. I don't need a bedroom, or even a bed. I'll gladly spend every night standing like a lamppost, on the stairs or at the back of the garden. I swear I don't need sleep at all, nobody says you absolutely have to sleep.

My Job

I am very indispensable at my job. My job is very indispensable. Not very many people are more indispensable than me. Not very many jobs are as indispensable as my job. Moreover, it is very hard. It's definitely a hard job. It takes a lot of energy. I give it everything I've got. I sit and stare. I drink coffee. I unfold my papers and shield them with my hand so nobody can spy on me. It wears you down. Not very many people understand that. That's why I have to rest so often. It's not for fun.

I Drive On

Every day I drive to the supermarket and back in an old banger. A Volkswagen from the late 1970s. It's a pile of rust, it's falling apart. I only use it for my short, daily drive.

I imagine the road crosses the USA. Five hundred kilometres of tarmac with prairie on either side. An exit to a motel with red doors. A fat woman dips bread in egg and milk and puts it on the pan. I fold my hands under the table and thank the Lord that we have made it this far without an accident, that we still have gas in the tank and oil in the engine. Outside the car is steaming.

My eyes are puffy from the sun. You eat with your elbow on the table, shovelling the food into your mouth. You're wearing white. It's getting dark, the air is cooler now. If I'm lucky, coyotes will run around out there tonight and howl. Then I turn towards you in the rickety bed. We got the last spare room, it's ugly, the wallpaper is in tatters.

Your hand is warm and dry, your eyes are closed. I lie there staring into space. There are brown stains on the ceiling, as though somebody had poured a cup of coffee upwards, and I wake you and ask if you think it's coffee. You think so. I wake you again because somebody is creeping around in the hall, probably the fat woman, and later I wake you again and offer you water. You have to make sure to drink enough, I say, and you drink and fall asleep again, and it's all right.

Because the next night you're the one who can't sleep. You lie and stare at me in another room, in another place; I'm exhausted from not having slept the night before. In this way we take turns staying awake, apart from the nights when neither of us can sleep. Every morning at five we drive off without paying the bill.

I sit in the car wearing a thin green dress with an hour-old embryo inside me. Little insects fly into the windshield; you turn on the wipers. The sun rises, and one day it's all over.

image: emma forsberg
<emma_forsberg@lycos.com>

Jackie Kay

Why Don't You Stop Talking

I saw her looking at me filling my trolley with chocolate biscuits. I weren't imagining things because she had one of them stuck-up looks on her face and I weren't having it. I've got too old to take any more crap. I know myself and I know other people. And I know when someone's coming over all judgemental. And she was. So I said to her, 'Life's too short to worry about having a fat arse.' She said, 'Sorry?' I said, 'You were looking in my trolley.' She looked around herself the way that people do when they've decided they are with a fruitcase, a total nutter. She walked off pushing her trolley down the aisle towards the bumper bags of crisps. But I weren't having it. You take enough, and one day you don't take no more. So I followed her with my trolley, nudged her in the elbow and I said to her, 'Watch your weight do you?' and she turned and said, 'Look, I wasn't looking at your biscuits for the reasons you think.' She were very well-spoken. I were shocked because she admitted she *was* looking into my trolley. I hadn't been imagining things. I knew I hadn't. She pushed her trolley away from me, but you can't leave me with a cliff-hanger like that. I followed her and said, 'What reasons then?' And she said, 'None of your business,' and walked off again rounding the corner to the long fridges. I saw her put some cottage cheese in her trolley and a tub of something.

I could tell she was a shy one. The shy don't talk enough. She was needing someone like me to coax her out of herself. I made sure I finished my shopping when she did and stood behind her in the checkout queue. It takes a lot for me to say sorry to anybody because nine times out of ten I am right. This time I decided I wanted to hear more and I said to her, 'Sorry about that earlier. It's the old paranoia.' She was loading her stuff onto the belt and her stuff was all very healthy. Tubs of cottage cheese. Bags of lettuce, spring onions, those tomatoes still on their vines, red apples, a small wrinkled melon and something weird I don't know the name of, but next time I come I might look for one and have it.

She flushed red in the face. She were quite a looker. The checkout girl was eyeing me suspiciously and looking uncomfortable. The shy one didn't reply. I waited but she didn't say nothing. I said to her, 'You don't look like a stuck-up cow, are you a stuck-up cow?' It were too late. It had just popped out my mouth and nothing stopping it. It's harder to take words back than it is to get a refund. The checkout girl looked at me frightened like as if I was carrying a gun. I could see that she were contemplating doing something like calling the Supermarket manager. The shy one looked straight at me, coolly and said, 'Why don't you stop talking?'

I have to admit she had a point there. I do have one of those tongues that gets me into a load of trouble. I can't help myself. I just come out with what's in my head and it has caused me terrible problems all my life. I don't know if it's just that it was the tongue I was born with and I couldn't do nothing about it or what. Sometimes it even feels like the words are not my decisions, like somebody else is talking with my tongue. Other times it feels like a big affliction like a hare lip or a cleft palate. I'd rather have a lisp, or a stutter. I wouldn't mind one of them bad stammers, then so much damage wouldn't be done cos the stammer would slow me down. She weren't the first one that has said that to me. I held up my hand and said, 'Fair enough, you want me to stop talking, but all I wanted to know was why you were looking in my trolley?'

She turned round quite vicious like, her beautiful looks all changed, her mouth snarling and she said to me. 'You're one of those people that just doesn't know when to stop. Get yourself a shrink.' I hadn't figured her for the nasty type somehow so that quite shocked me. I'd thought she was nice. I didn't usually get people so wrong. My big breasts felt suddenly bigger and I crossed my arms in front of myself. Actually I wanted to ram my trolley into the backs of her rayon nylon tights, but I can exercise control when I want to. I'm never violent with my fists. She packed her healthy stuff. She had some order to the way she was doing it. And then she left. I had to load my ten packets of chocolate Hobnobs, my three packs of Jaffas, my Penguins, my Kitkats and my two packs of mini chocolate rolls onto the conveyor belt and give the girl a look that said 'What are you looking at?' so as she would keep it belted. I didn't say nothing to her but I was dying to tell her how that stuck-up cow was in the wrong and I was in the right. The times I am silent when I need to talk is as hard as bursting for a piss. I can feel the talk coming and it's like a physical thing. I rushed outside and talked to myself behind the recycling bins where nobody could see me except an old alkie who was rummaging through some discarded bottles which hadn't made it inside either the brown or the green or the white bins. He was swallowing the dregs of wine and rainwater from green bottles and he hardly paid me any attention at all. His trousers were wet at the front.

All the way home that sentence of hers was right in my head and I said it to myself out loud. When I were four I was staying at my Nan's for a few days while my mum was in hospital. I was talking away to my Nan about the little friend I'd found one day in the square of green outside her high-rise flat in Hackney. The little girl was wearing bright red trousers and red wellie boots. I told my Nan how I'd gone again down to the square of green and she'd disappeared and she was funny because she'd been telling me her sister was a 'whiny little swine' and I'd never heard somebody as little as me say 'swine.' Suddenly my Nan said to me, 'Thelma, stop the yabbering and the blabbering, you're tiring me out you are,' and I was shocked, but I kept on telling her all about the girl. How she was smaller in height than me and how she had carrot colour hair and where did my Nan think she had gone. I'd been looking for her every day now for ages. How could my Nan find her? My Nan said, 'Right, that does it, I'll have to fetch the Red Loony Van Men. The Red Loony Van Men will come for you and take you to the Asylum, to the Mental Home where you'll learn to hold that tongue of yours.' And to my total horror, she got up and put on her Mackintosh, doing the buttons as fast as she could manage, and put her triangle of patterned scarf over her head, tying it tightly, no-nonsense like, under her chin and left the house. I watched her from the window, small and definite below me. I were in a right state. I imagined the inside of the Red Loony Van: there would be cruel-eyed men with ropes to tie me up and Alsatians to keep guard. I can remember it exactly as if I'd actually been bundled into the back of it. My Nan were strict but I still loved her like nothing else. I slept with her when I were there in her big high bed. I cried looking down at her as I watched her disappear up the street. She came back half an hour later with a fish supper but by that time the Red Loony Van Men were taking up the whole of my head and I couldn't eat and I were silent for some time. She might have regretted what she'd done cos she kept saying, 'What's the matter with you, cat got your tongue?'

All my family use to talk a lot except my Nan and my silent brother. He hardly spoke but then that was because he had nothing in his head. My mother talked a lot. You couldn't get a word in with her. And she could be vicious with her tongue. I'd rather she'd hit me than have heard the half of what she said to me. My dad talked with his hands and his mouth when he was around. My dad was from Jamaica and my mum were a real East Ender. I don't see them anymore and they don't see each other. One Christmas we all said things we shouldn't and once they were said we couldn't get over them. I reckon families should be banned. They should find some other way of doing it.

I was feeling rattled and when I'm feeling rattled the thoughts speed up inside my head and I can't get any peace. I walked towards the Tube, I can't walk fast because I'm carrying a fat arse. I laughed to myself, swinging it down the High Street. The litter was blowing this way and that and the place was filthy. Somebody ought to clear this street up. It's a disgrace. I stopped to get some money out from the wall with my card.

I were just getting my card out when this big geezer pushed in, jumping the queue. I said to him, 'I was here first.' He said, 'You were mucking about with your handbag, I'm in a hurry.' I could tell the geezer looked the dangerous type because he had a bad face, but that didn't stop me. If I feel wronged, I have to speak up. Simple as that. You can't go about life letting people get away with things. I said, 'You know what's wrong with you don't you? You got no manners. Have you always been like that pushing in front of women? Did your mother not teach you no manners? I'm talking to you.' He was checking his balance. I was standing quite close to him. I could see he had a lot more money than me. 'You think cos you're rich you can jump queues?' I said to him. He turned round taking his notes and putting them in his wallet. He had broad shoulders. 'You're lucky I have got manners,' he said to me. 'If I didn't I'd belt you one on that fat black mouth of yours!' He got into his black car which he'd parked half on the pavement on double yellow lines. I shouted at his car, 'I'll report you asshole!' I were shaking again.

Get yourself home Thelma. Get yourself home. Some days are just sent to try you. As soon as you get up you know it's going to be giving it to you all day. I was trying to walk quickly and puffing and sweating. All of a sudden, I didn't feel safe. The sun was shining for a change but it wasn't making me happy. People can't really cope with the heat in this country. They bake and they sweat and they wear the wrong things. I noticed an ice cream cone lying on the street melting. It was her voice I heard first. It were so loud and shrill. I told myself to walk on but I couldn't help but notice that she was shaking her child, back and forth, on the street, really shaking him like he were a rag doll. She was a young woman. I can't stand nobody being unkind to kids, so I said to her. 'Easy does it love, he's just a little fellow.' I was trying to be careful and not antagonize the woman. She stared at me with her mouth full open as if she hadn't heard right, then she said, 'Mind your own fucking business. He's not just a little fellow, he's a fucking psychopath, he's been winding me up all day and he fucking knows it. Don't you?' She said turning her attentions to the little guy again and jabbing him while he screamed red in the face. I never heard of anyone accusing a two-year-old of being a psycho. I said to her, 'You must just be stressed out. Don't take it out on him. What can he do?' She thought I'd gone cos she whirled back around to me, turning her head away from the screaming toddler who was now giving it big licks. 'Beat it!' she shouted at me. 'Shut your fucking trap!'

It was something I'd been noticing more and more on the

London streets. How many mothers swear these days, really bad swearing. Not just bloody and damn. But Cs and Fs and stuff. I said to her, 'You ought to wash out your mouth, swearing like that in front of your kid!' Out it came, I couldn't help myself. I saw her coming. She came right up to me, still holding the toddler in one arm. She slapped my face really hard so that it stung. The toddler stopped crying all of a sudden. She said, 'I told you to shut it. Who do you think you are you fat interfering cow?' She was skinny and wiry and had sharp features like a fox. She was pushing me with one hand as she spoke, rhythmic like. She was strong too. Strong arms, must train at the gym. I was scared she was going to knock me right down. I said, 'I was only trying to help.' She stopped pushing. 'Help? Don't kid yourself. You don't know what I've been through this morning. Piss off before I kick the shit out of your fat arse.' I walked off, quite shaken up I was, my arse swinging, indignant. When I'd got a few hundred yards away from her I shouted, 'You need help. You should get yourself a shrink!' I could never resist having the last word, me. I hadn't bargained on her running though, fast as she did, the boy still bundled up in her arms.

I slipped into Boots and hid beside the Nappies. I were having some day of it, no mistake. I were totally out of breath; just trying to breathe normal hurt my chest. I tried to slow down my thumping ticker. The sweat was pouring down me, especially between my breasts. I bought some Tampax Super Plus while I was about it because I was sure my time of month was upon me. Because I always get into trouble with my tongue and strangers around my time of month. I live on me own, so there's nobody to shout at in the house. I used to have a boyfriend and I would rant at him for hours, and one day he just packed his bags and left. I were better off without him anyway because he just got on my nerves. It were only because he had a car that I tolerated him for a bit. It were handy when we did the Supermarket shopping. I went out into the street, keeping a sharp eye out for the screaming mother. There are so many mad people in London now. You've really got to watch your back. I know my tongue is going to get me killed by one of those total tulips one day. I think I was already thinking about what I need to do.

I got on the tube, Piccadilly line. I stared at the faces of the people in the tube. Some were reading newspapers, some books, some just staring straight ahead like me. Some had been at work and smelled and were dirty. Some had been shopping. I turned to the girl sitting next to me who looked friendly. I said, 'You won't believe the day I've had!' I could tell she didn't want me to go into it because she looked panic-stricken. People often look like that when I talk to them as if I'm trapping them or something when I'm only trying to be friendly. I decided to say no more to her. Instead I gave a look, rolling my eyes to indicate my day. She smiled a bit and looked the other way.

I climbed up the four flights of stairs to my council flat in Woodberry Down, off Manor Road. The stairs kill me every time. I switched on the telly when I got into my flat. I can't stand silence all by itself. It was that silly cow that encourages people to slag each other off. The only thing I like about her is that she is fat. I like fat people a whole lot better than thin people. Actually I've noticed a lot of differences between the fat and the thin. The fats are more generous with their cash and their emotions. The thin are more mean and sly. The fat are talkers and the thin are silent. The fat laugh more. The strangest thing of all is when it comes to people who are off their rocker. A thin mad person is worse than a fat one. A thin mad silent type is lethal. Think of all the serial killers and psychopaths and murderers – they've mostly been thin and silent.

Just because I talk a lot people think I'm mad. I hate those silent people that let you talk on and on till you've run yourself into the ground and are left with egg on your face. They leave you repeating yourself while they listen and nod saying their few chosen words because they can choose because they weren't born with the misfortune of having a tongue like mine. I always finish off by saying something stupid like, 'Well I just thought it was out of order,' and when they don't say anything, I say, 'Well I just thought it was out of order,' and then I'll have to trail off because they still haven't said anything. They like their little pauses. I'm always falling into their pauses. They are like traps, or shafts. I fall down into the dark, shouting. It's not the talkers that have the power; it's the silent ones. They're the ones that rule the world. Just look around.

I put the kettle on and make myself a big mug of tea. I open my biscuits and put six on a tea plate for myself. I can't get that woman in the supermarket out of my head. Out of all the trying things today, she's the one that's done my head in. I reckon she was looking in my trolley because she's anorexic or bulimic or something. Well you don't know the half of quiet people; they keep so much hidden.

When I were young most of my friends were shy. I always liked shy people. True, they didn't talk a lot, until they opened up and then there was no stopping them, but they actually liked me, talking, they liked having me around chatting nineteen to the dozen because I covered for them. Their shyness didn't show if they were with me. If they weren't with me, they'd have to blush and stumble and stuff. But what I really started to notice about the shy was the amount of secrets they had, secrets and grudges and all sorts. I were totally amazed. You'd never imagine how much could be lurking there, under that blushing face, you'd never imagine how much the shy needed revenge. So it makes me wonder about her, that woman. Maybe she told me to see a shrink because she's actually seeing one. You never know. It's possible. Let's face it, it is not normal to go staring for ages into someone's trolley. She were trying to make out that I was the one who weren't normal, but it was her. It was her all along.

Some bloke is screaming at his girlfriend on the telly and the girlfriend is crying and what's her face is wandering around with her microphone. What a world. I eat one Hobnob after another. I've got so jangled that only my biccies will calm me down. I need a sugar surge or something.

I go into my bathroom and put my tongue out in front of the mirror. It is pink and thick and long and slightly speckled like a bird's egg, but other than that it just looks like an ordinary tongue. You wouldn't suspect it of nothing. I lift it up using my muscles and look underneath the tongue. Again, nothing doing really. A bit gross seeing all the joins of the tongue, stretchy, sinewy, slimy strings. All my life I've been told by so many different people: 'That tongue of yours will get you into trouble one day.' And all my life it has. I'm constantly living on my tongue's edge. I can't afford to take no more risks. Every time my tongue gets me into trouble, it will be punished. Then it will soon learn. I pick up the razor and I cut my tongue. It is actually painful, but the pain feels good. The pain feels deserved. The blood is generous and very red and it pours down my face. I wish they could all see me now.

image: kathy acker by kasia boddy

Kasia Boddy

Interview with Kathy Acker

This interview took place in Acker's flat in London in September 1997. She died in November of the same year.

Kasia Boddy: In an interview published after you lived in London in the 1980s, you said that you felt both the lack of a literary underground in Britain and felt misunderstood by the British press. Can you say more about that, especially now that you've come back? Is this still true?

Kathy Acker: I don't think you have an underground here. By underground I don't mean young writers who aren't known yet. What I mean is a recognizable alternative to what we call commercial literature, that is really as public as anything else. And no, I don't think you have that.

Boddy: You missed it?

Acker: It's changed here, so now I'm talking about how I felt back then. I felt that it was easier for a writer to get published here, especially for a writer who was slightly, or more than slightly, unconventional. But you couldn't go too far because there was no underground. William Burroughs would never have survived here, and certainly wasn't published here until he was famous enough. In the States there is a true underground, in which people like Burroughs of course are published. It was both good and bad. In one way, it was easier for writers here, and in another way it was harder, because you had to stay somewhat within the norm.

Boddy: So you stood out.

Acker: Well, I was American. It's very different. And I was brought over with a big bang. Sonny Mehta, who was head of Picador at the time, did a number and for whatever reason things caught on. They had never seen – 'they', the English – had never seen anything like *Blood and Guts in High School*, but I don't think that there was ever any sense of where I came from. I was seen as a loner. There was more of a cult around my image, around my personality, than there was interest in my writing. And certainly there was no interest in where the writing fitted in in any history of writing. The sectors of the American underground that I come from are fairly well-known in most countries – most people know about the Black Mountain poets, or the art scene. Process writing would mean something. They just don't mean very much here.

Boddy: Why do you think that is?

Acker: I don't know. This is just a guess. There is a position that literature has in English society that really has to do with 'properness', with class. One speaks properly: whatever the subject matter, the elegance and the proper use of irony shows that one fits properly, one upholds the class structure. There is something different with the Irvine Welsh thing, but then I wonder. The Scottish writers – like James Kelman and Alasdair Gray – are closer to American writers. So there are ties. There is a certain network. There're very few writers here [in England] . . . Ballard, but that's very peculiar, Iain Sinclair – who's very well known to the American scene – and some poets.

Boddy: So how did you fit in?

Acker: I don't think I did. I was seen as the oddball wild woman. So I was fitted into places that said 'we like wild women.' To my mind I was in a little cage in the zoo that instead of 'monkey' said 'female American radical'. So whenever they wanted the female American radical to comment on anything, to make a token appearance, they'd pull me out of the cage and give me some money. It was quite lucrative, I must say.

Boddy: How have things changed now?

Acker: England on the whole has got very American and I think the publishing industry has changed a great deal. When they consider now if they'll take a book, trendiness is the name of the game. I'm not sure it's better to tell you the truth. On the one hand, I like the way Irvine Welsh and friends have gone against proper language. On the other hand, there's a kind of interest in surface spark, surface lightening, and little interest in anything else. It's very conservative in a way. I think literature is deeply about lineage, and there is nothing to do with lineage here. Basically it's realist writing. OK, so it's grungy realist writing and it talks about toilets or dope.

Boddy: In the Nelson Algren tradition?

Acker: Well I take Algren to be not just a realist. I love Algren. Next to Faulkner he's my favourite.

Boddy: In *In Memoriam* you speak of Faulkner as 'the American writer'. What is it about Faulkner that makes him 'the American'?

Acker: First of all, there weren't any novelists around then who weren't just realists. The way I see it is that it starts off with Hawthorne and Melville – you have Cooper on one side, the realist telling fairy tales (realism has always looked like fairy tales, even Dickens). For me, the American novel starts off with Hawthorne, Melville, Poe – and it's not a novel, it's a reaction to the novel, it's a romance. The novel, as Roland Barthes would say, is deeply about bourgeois life. Hawthorne and Melville and Poe are revolutionaries in lots of ways. So you have the novel in America starting off being radical, not being real. Just in literary terms, the fight is against realism. *Moby Dick* is not a realist novel, and *Pierre* just makes fun of the whole idea – it's the first genre-fuck novel. But then you don't really have the tradition continuing. You go through a lot of radical writing that is mainly poetry. And nobody is that interesting until Faulkner, who just shines. He does something interesting – he does a novel that is both realist and radical. He keeps narrative and yet it's absolutely radical. What I take to be radical is that interest in America in something called guts – a heart. What does Poe say? That if you wrote the truth of the heart you'd set the whole world on fire. It's like fuck you, the rules, that's what you do. That's what Faulkner did. Algren's like that for me, but I can't think of anyone else.

Boddy: What about Stein?

Acker: I don't think of her as a novelist.

Boddy: What about *The Making of Americans*?

Acker: Well, you definitely get the experimental novel. And you have Djuna Barnes – *Nightwood* is totally radical.

Boddy: Lots of people have acknowledged your own influence.

Acker: Oh yes and the academic industry on me is getting fairly large.

Boddy: What do think you've given other writers? Do you notice that influence?

Acker: I think I've freed other writers. I think it's different with men and women. But I broke rules. I said you've just got to write however you want to write. What's said to me most often is that people felt freed by my writing to do what they want to do rather than what they were told to do. Here I'm guessing, but I think for women, there's this real empowerment. Coming out of sixties and seventies feminism, women so felt that they had to write in certain ways, that they couldn't talk about certain things, have certain attitudes. I think I gave a lot of women the freedom to say 'I can still be strong and yet I can talk about this.' I can see the influence most strongly with women. Dennis Cooper is another. We are about the only writers of our generations who crossed over, who didn't compromise at all, but crossed over to some extent.

Boddy: Your recent work seems more interested in the idea of its audience than perhaps it used to be. Is that fair?

Acker: I'm more interested in narrative – that's for sure. Being ill, having the cancer, has changed a great deal for me. So I'm rethinking everything yet again. In some ways it's just a continuation of my work. The cancer wasn't devastating; it was more like a fabulous school which I went to where I learned a lot. I don't know how all that is going to come out.

Boddy: You've always rejected the idea of writing as self-expression.

Acker: I've certainly said that. On the other hand, I've always felt that you have to write what you have to write. I don't have an idea of a reader out there in my best moments. That's certainly true of what I'm writing right now. I write what I have to write. And then there are the moments – because you can't do that every day – when you're doing your technique stuff, theory. But you just have to do what's coming through you. In that way, I'm close to Robert Duncan who talked a lot about inspiration and the muse. I do a lot of drafts and I certainly think of the reader towards the final drafts. I make my money still by performing and I can't afford to lose audiences. So I can't afford to have too many chapters in a book that I can't read aloud.

Boddy: What do you do in that revision?

Acker: I first of all make it clear what the intent is. They may or may not be interested but at least they can get it. This will be about this problem and you will all get it. There is a certain clarity that is necessary, even in the most experimental of texts. I didn't think this when I was younger, but now I think there is a kind of pacing. You can't go too fast for a reader. You can't have too many characters or people won't be sure who the characters are. Technical stuff!

Boddy: What do you mean by pacing? You've spoken before of breath.

Acker: I read all my texts out loud as a final draft. In terms of breath, I mean the same thing that poets mean. I was trained by poets, not by novelists.

Boddy: The idea of the line seems central to poetry.

Acker: With me too.

Boddy: How does that work in prose?

Acker: Let me get a copy of *Pussy* and I'll show you. [She reads the beginning of the abortion sequence p.79] You see how the rhythm works. I hear the very simple rhythm. It goes for the jokes. It's a very straightforward, limpid rhythm that will close up at the moment you want to close the meaning. But it won't do so obtrusively. I can see the rhythm is almost transparent. Whereas something like Antigone's Diary . . . [She reads the beginning of that section, p.163] So it's that long sentence which just gets the anger out. That to me is a very oral rhythm where you get the emotion of who the person is – as opposed to the transparent rhythm where there is no emotion, no character. And there are times when there is something like a poetic rhythm. This is from the second chapter; this is what Louise Vanaen writes to the whores. [She reads from pp.30-31] So there it gets to depending on each word and sentence. It's more poetical.

Boddy: Do you think when people read to themselves they get these rhythms?

Acker: People say to me it's very different to hear me read aloud.

Boddy: William Gass has said that he doesn't want his readers to speed-read and so he tries to slow them down. How do you slow the reader down?

Acker: You just increase the tension in language. The first section I read is very open language and you read it fast. The more poetic it becomes, the more density there is, you slow it down.

Boddy: It's also punctuation.

Acker: Well, a comma's a breath, and a sentence is a thought, and a paragraph is an emotion. This is just pure Charles Olson. You're always working the paragraph against the sentence.

Boddy: Writing your work to be read aloud means in some ways you are emulating the techniques of oral storytelling.

Acker: I think I'm totally into storytelling. My interest in narrative is an interest in myth. That's what I do: tell stories. I don't just tell one story, I tell lots of stories and they all intertwine. I mean now, in the later novels. I have very little interest in writing that isn't about storytelling; what I read is mainly storytelling. But it's an oral tradition.

Boddy: In his 1934 essay 'The Storyteller', Walter Benjamin claimed that storytelling was dying out.

Acker: I think now the novel is dying out, and the big questions are, what is needed? What is necessary? The novel is irrelevant in a way.

Boddy: Benjamin linked storytelling with community life; the novel was the genre of solitary individuals.

Acker: Now people don't have the kind of lives where they sit and read a novel. Except the most commercial stuff which you read on a plane just to get through the plane ride. Which is when most people read novels. But there is a real need for performative stuff, for oral stuff. In America the oral tradition is huge now, the spoken word is very lively. Dennis [Cooper] is very involved in all that stuff.

Boddy: Does the net provide a kind of community?

Acker: I think there was a golden age of the net when people were suddenly just allowed to write and they wrote incredible amounts of stuff. People felt free to write however they pleased,

One thing that doesn't go on the net is punctuation, proper grammar. I think it's all changing; the Net's changing. Right now all the publishers want all the rights whenever you do anything for them. And the reason is that they want Net rights. What are they going to do with them? I never sell net rights. I put everything up on the web page. But I think Grove can go fuck it. They're not going to make money out of net rights. But they just want to own what you do outright.

Boddy: You've described yourself as coming out of a poetry tradition – the Black Mountain poets who were all concerned with finding individual voices. You've said that you moved away from them because you couldn't find your own voice, you didn't have a voice. Now your novels are certainly recognizable as yours. Do you think you have a voice, or is style different from voice?

Acker: I guess something's developed that sounds like me. I would say it's narrowed. I can't answer that. I think I'm probably fairly identifiable, but I don't know what it is. For me, voice meant 'I want to express this' – what Jerome Rothenberg thought voice meant was that 'this is my stance in the world, and therefore I'm going to write the piece from this stance.' I think that was what I was revolting against. Do I think that I have a certain stance? Probably one's developed because there certainly is a kind of history now. I think the main problem when I write is that you get into these troughs where it is too easy, you've done it already and could easily do it again. Worse than that is that you build up expectations.

Boddy: How do you resist that?

Acker: God. You just have to search for new material that's free, that hasn't been touched. That's difficult, because it is so easy to go where you've gone before and it's such a bad mistake.

Boddy: I was at Brighton two years ago when you spoke about 'languages of the body' that you find, which you distinguished from language about the body.

Acker: I little knew how that idea would escalate, that is all I can say! That's what my whole life has become, because that's what the cancer was – literally language coming out through the body. It was totally transformative in that way. That's what I'm writing about now. I don't know how to say this theoretically – the connections between my body, language and meaning, if you like, myth or narrative. One thing I learned working with cancer is – and we're talking metaphorically now – that it's as if there are different emanations. Only the physical emanations are visible, and behind the physical lies what's called the emotional body. You can regard cancer as a physical disease and treat it accordingly, or you can go back and search for the roots of it in the emotional, causal body. It has to do with various turnings of meanings and it has to do with how energy works. So suddenly story, meaning and energy are very closely intertwined. Now we don't think that really because we are big old rationalists; we think story basically doesn't exist – it's something we make up. But to find out that story lies there behind material reality is something incredible. For instance, I have this parasite thing – I haven't been able to get well – and then I realized that the thing that led to it was an incident that, for whatever reasons, was like a little window to something that happened before I was born – that is my father left my mother before I was born. And suddenly I saw the reason I wasn't getting well. I thought what was it to be in my mother's womb and have my mother lose her husband. I think it is what Benjamin meant when he was thinking of Karl Krauss, by 'breath', or 'in the beginning was the word.' In the beginning was meaning. I've been reading Emerson and the last line of Emerson's journal is 'causality is perfect'; it all means something. And that is absolutely antithetical to what we've been taught; we don't really think it means anything. The novel's all based on you making it up? I'm finding the opposite. You don't make it up. It's sitting there. The universe is meaning.

Boddy: How does what you are doing, not necessarily now but in the past, link to modernist writing about the body? A sense that when other value systems break down there is a refuge in the body, in sexuality. Do you feel a connection?

Acker: Absolutely. I think that is an ongoing tradition. The turn to sexuality is a basic. That's very American, I think – that kind of physicality. Emerson, Thoreau's body in nature, Margaret Fuller saying the best thing is waves. I work with my fascinations and sometimes I don't know why I'm fascinated, and I've always been fascinated with sexuality. Some of the time I was just goofing or parodying; I wasn't trying to find a meaning there until the later work. I guess that alternative tradition in America is very strong. Sex is something very weird in Britain. It's always seen as something satanic.

Boddy: How much is coming to language through the body like automatic writing?

Acker: It's about language and the body. Coming through the body can also just mean speech; it doesn't have to mean cut-up or poetic. If you hear it, it's coming through the body.

Boddy: The Surrealist experiments with automatic language were all to do with the mind and the unconscious, rather than the body.

Acker: To an extent I was influenced by the Surrealists but they were Descartians. They were Freudians; they weren't interested in the body. The body deals with narratives. I don't mean stories. The knee gets hurt and then it gets better.

Boddy: Narrative is about chronology, which was one of the things surrealism rejected. It was also a rejection of rationalism.

Acker: Which was really valuable, and a lot of their experiments were certainly behind a lot of the stuff I learned as a kid.

Boddy: Do you see a turning point in your work, from destroying, in some way, to building?

Acker: I think it's both building and finding meaning. The way I think of it now, and I guess I'm totally influenced by having gone through all this stuff, is that you don't build – because that puts you in the position of maker – but you find. You free the energy, and in that way you build. That's what literature would do; that's the old idea of catharsis. That's one of the well-springs of literature for us – that it's the healing that's done prior to the ceremony. That's what those Greek dramas were. One thing literature can do is healing. It's the old stuff – prior to the novel.

Boddy: How much is the finding of meaning individual and how much is it something like the Jungian idea of tapping in to archetypes?

Acker: I've been reading Jung all summer. I haven't put this together theoretically at all. If you're asking how individuality fits into all this, we're probably going to posit a whole other idea of what it is to be a self and the self /other relationship. In this way the work Blanchot and Bataille did was seminal. Blanchot, talking of Bataille, shows how consciousness comes from intercourse with another person. We're going to find that we're related to each other in ways that we didn't imagine. I certainly don't question individuality. Reading this book about Emerson and his friends, I was thinking how writers really come in clumps – not that there's a group soul, but there are certainly times when energy is there, and other times when it doesn't exist.

Boddy: Do you feel then that you're part of a clump? Of a group?

Acker: I do and I don't. I feel very close to two writers – to Iain Sinclair and to Jeanette Winterson. I feel that we are on the same wavelength. I feel very close to the healing community. There are writers I am close to in America, but they are not novelists.

Boddy: Would you define your books as novels?

Acker: To tell you the truth, not terribly. They are big chunks of prose. But are they novels? More groups of stories. Some of them aren't even that. Somewhat philosophical treatises. They're hotchpotches, aren't they? I don't know how you'd define them.

They're romances. They're really that American strange thing. Melville was always my great hero.

Boddy: You describe yourself sometimes as a pirate – finding things, taking things – but also as an explorer. Explorers discover new places whereas pirates always go where someone else has been. Are these two roles different?

Acker: They're not different for me because everything under the sun starts from stuff that's left. I don't see how you go somewhere new without going through detritus, garbage. You have to find ways of understanding the thing or you won't come back. What did Cixous say about Moses? Most people who go into the wilderness don't come back; they're transformed. To come back there has to be something of the old system of meaning. Otherwise how can Moses talk to the people?

Boddy: What have you taken with you in your explorations into say the languages of the body?

Acker: In my case, I'm really linked to certain lineages. I'm a very traditional writer in certain ways. I come so definitely out of Burroughs and Miller and that group of writers. You can see where I'm coming from. I go my own steps further – added a bit of theory, added a bit of Black Mountain poetry. If you're asking what I take with me, I couldn't have done what I've done, whatever that is, if I hadn't come out of those lineages.

Boddy: It's a very male tradition.

Acker: Extremely.

Boddy: The only woman you talk about in your book of essays, *Bodies of Work*, is Colette.

Acker: Those essays are just what people asked me to write. But it's true, I do come out of male traditions very strongly. Men have had the power, the language, the voice.

Boddy: Yet there have been many women writers, and women's traditions. Was there something there that you didn't want?

Acker: Well, the feminist sixties and seventies turned me off because it was really strident. What I was given when I was growing up as the women's tradition of writing was fairly staid realist writing. Ellen Friedman, when she published that book *Breaking the Sequence* about radical women writing, she turned me on quite a bit. Until then I didn't think it through, but it's very obvious that the strong radical tradition in America in prose is female. But that's not the accepted story. Especially after *The Madwoman in the Attic*, because that book was the canon, and everyone thought the most radical you'd get was Willa Cather. I actually like Willa Cather a great deal. But that's it. I grew up hating that stuff. I'd rather be one of the bad boys than be a good girl. Feminism, when I grew up, was restrictive. I remember going to them in the early days and saying 'hi, here's my writing,' and them saying 'you're a man, get out of here.' I just didn't fit at all.

Boddy: Some critics argue that non-linear writing – breaking the sequence – is particularly female – that women don't live linear lives, think linearly as men do. Do you agree that a particular way of writing like that can be particularly male or female?

Acker: I wonder if there is a woman's experience? I would say that if I thought of anything being a woman's experience it would be like Cixous talking about the spectre. And the spectre talks about stealing. And she says the thing is to steal and not know you're doing anything wrong. It would be to just to write the way you do and not know how radical it was. What would women's writing be like? I guess that part of me does feel that there is this flow that's spiral and undulating and has to do with female writing. It comes down to the question of whether there are essentially women and men. What would non-difference look like?

Boddy: In *Written on the Body*, Jeanette Winterson explored the idea of androgynous language. Do you think there can be androgynous language, language without gender?

Acker: Actually I don't think so. I know Jeanette thinks so and I wonder if she's preserving certain territory when she says that. I used to think so until last time I was pregnant. I knew it was the last time I was ever going to have a chance to be pregnant. There was no way I could keep the child. It was a very painful abortion, emotionally, and it made me think that, like it or not, there is a very deep way in which we are connected to wombs, to child-bearing. It's there. One can't discount the physical. I have friends now who are changing genders and I know it's very big. I know there are probably mid-genders, but in my experience there is something about having a womb that can't be discounted.

Boddy: Do you think you can identify a piece of writing as being by a woman?

Acker: No, I don't at all. Partly what a novelist does is write in another's voice. We don't write ourselves. Henry James is one of the great writers of women. In that way I agree with Jeanette that the writer is truly androgynous. The writer is a channeler. In a way, the writer doesn't exist; you're as good as what comes through you, and God knows what comes through you. I guess I think both – that there is something about having a certain body, and maybe that has its imprint on the writing, but there is also the fact that one isn't writing oneself. Although in the transmitting, one is writing a self.

Boddy: I was reading an interview in which you described *In Memoriam* as a turning point in your writing, that before that form was determined by theory, and that now form was 'coming more organically in the sense that it's based on theme'.

Acker: I did an interview with Iain Sinclair and Iain said it very precisely: that what you do when you write is go out and find. You're looking for the story and you find it. It's organic in the way that you're not making the story up; the story is already there and you're letting it come through.

Boddy: And the form in which the story comes is in some way natural?

Acker: It's in whatever it's in.

Boddy: Do you think your earlier work was imposing forms on stories?

Acker: No, I think I've always written this way. I don't think I ever imposed a form. I've always written organically, except for *Kathy goes to Haiti* – that was totally different, there was nothing organic about that book. I just wanted to write a porn novel so I could make money. It was a calculated grab for money, and I lost. There was a porn company which was giving poets eight hundred dollars for a porn novel. All my friends had done one, and I thought I could use eight hundred dollars. So I went ahead and it was really boring. I got totally bored and I started making jokes and messing around. But it was planned. By organic, I mean it forms itself as it proceeds, as opposed to you sit down and you plan it out.

Boddy: Do you think you've always been more interested in form than content?

Acker: I've always thought more about form than content. I never thought about content. And now? Probably not. It's hard to think about content. Now it's just voices, I look for the energy. I'm a process writer; that's all I've ever meant.

Boddy: What's the new book?

Acker: God knows. I'm just starting it. I was going to write a book about healing and I got through the introduction and about fifty pages and thought, I really hate non-fiction, I'm totally bored. Why write about what you know already? So I thought it does have to be fiction, but I definitely want to use a lot of the material. It's great material. I've written quite a bit, but the beginning is just starting.

Boddy: The humour in your work is something that I think tends to be overlooked.

Acker: I think my sense of humour is very black. It's goofy. For me to write and be satisfied, there has to be something outrageous. I have to have the feeling that nobody could possibly do this, it's too stupid. And then I feel comfortable with it.

Boddy: So it's not that you're trying to shock?

Acker: No, I don't have a sense of an audience that would be shocked. I live in my own baby crib to a large extent. When I first came over here and all these people were shocked, I was in shock! It's just words, what's your problem?! I had been in New York and I was in a baby crib with poets and artists, and they're not shocked. I had no sense that what I was doing was shocking.

Boddy: Is that something that distinguishes writing today from earlier avant-garde work – that it's no longer possible to shock?

Acker: My stuff still upsets people. I can't get *Pussy* published in this country. Looking for junk down toilet bowels is OK, but girls having good sex isn't!

Boddy: To get back to the idea of humour . . .

Acker: I think I've got a quirky sense of humour. The beginning of *Blood and Guts in High School*, making it about a father and daughter, was just my idea of a joke. Basically it was stuff to do with the break-up of my second marriage and I thought it was really boring – I do think of an audience! – so I thought I'll make it about a father and daughter, that's more interesting. That's just my sense of 'why not?' I didn't mean anything. Underlying it there was a great deal of myth about fathers and daughters, but it was just a bad joke.

Boddy: And no one got the joke!

Acker: No. No one even thought it was funny. Everyone was asking me about deep meaning. In San Francisco a lot of the dykes came out of incestuous homes and a number had told me 'you were the first person to write about it!' I think my novels are bloody goofy. I don't think *In Memoriam* is terribly funny, and *My Mother Demonology* is kind of a serious book. But I think there are sections in *Empire of the Senseless* that are goofy – the last section. I get on a roll. I thought in *Pussy*, the girls are goofy, and all the rat stuff. And everyone got very shocked – 'Oh, these girls are so dirty. They're such violent, filthy girls.' I just thought it was fun. I had a good time writing that. After all they're pirates. It was just a boys' book I turned into a girls' book. I was ripping off *Treasure Island* obviously, and I really thought *Pussy* was less violent. There is a scene in *Treasure Island* where there's an actual killing and I turned it into a girl throwing a stone at another girl. When it came to girls, it didn't feel that right to be that violent, although God knows, I know enough cases of lesbian battery. People get offended awfully easily, I think. Even the bloody queen who writes the astrology column in the *Bay Times* went on a rant about how of course he didn't believe in banning books, except in one case – mine!

Boddy: What do you think of the way publishing has latched on to identity politics to market books?

Acker: Identity politics took over the States. Very dangerous. I think it's repulsive. Even though it comes out of postmodernism, it's a backlash to postmodernism. I can see the point. I can see why 'ye olde' black lesbian wants to assert black lesbianism – for all sorts of political reasons. But I think that you have to be really careful that when you're asserting identity you're only asserting in a certain time and place, and that you don't make an absolute. And writing, novel writing, just isn't about that. It can be for a moment. If you're going to just write about yourself, you have to do what Emerson and Thoreau did, and go through the I to something else – something deeper. You have to end up somewhere that doesn't just go 'today I went to the bathroom five times and ate an apple.' I think that my work is extremely difficult given this sign of the times because I don't fit into any identity. I can't be marketed as gay, I don't even look good in the feminist sections, and yet I'm not 'ye olde straight novelist'. There's no way to categorize the writing.

Stella Duffy
STICK FIGURES

The stick is the most glorious signifier. Yes, she has been far more ill than this. Standing on death's door, suitcase in her hand, a songbook compendium of how close to the very far. Or other times, not physically ill but worse – heartsick. The pumping organ of possibility shattered and bleeding and inexplicably pumping still. Pushing through the life-giving blood regardless, when all she wanted from life-giving was to give it away. She has been far more far gone than this. She has sat in the bright-lit pit of despair and known darkness was never coming back to offer fake-death solace. Today though, she is the victim of average muscle spasm, ordinary back ruination. After weeks of too much fun, at the end-of-joy-times, she walks with a stick.

The stick is useful, last night she used two to climb the stairs. One her own, the other a hand-me-down legacy from her grandmother's death, the stick turned chalice, its host of heavy memories was so full. Climbing the stairs with those two was a hazardous ascent, suburban K2. Today she uses just the one, her own. A painted walnut stick, straight and solid but light, plastic handle ending in a dragon-head mould, a gift on her thirtieth birthday. Joke gift, comedy present, and yet so useful. Too useful. Too damn necessary. But that is just the background, the how-to of getting here. And it is the point of now that matters, more than the past passing of arrival.

Now, she stands on the threshold of the foyer, helped from the car, the partner-as-driver speeding off to find free parking in time for the drinks and chocolate purchases that are the only way to get through these next hours. And the stick-bearer is left alone for the first time in seven days. She takes a trembling step. The steps are trembling, the pain is real. And she holds the stick before her. It is not noticed at first, the lights are dim at the entrance, the queue for programmes and sweets lengthy, the milling children stand in the way of the dragon's head she clasps surprisingly comfortably in her right hand. But then with a step-limp-step she moves into the body of the room, the double-size ceiling, a mezzanine of watchers ready to look. Just in case, just in case she is someone who matters. She is not. But something about her does. And the stick sweeps all before it. It creates a path. Watchful fathers pull heedless children from before her, teenage girls turn shuffled backs, old ladies offer sympathetic glances. Sympathetic and not a little curious. She is not an old lady. But she is surely ill.

The stick is a wand, conjuring stories in those around her. The old men bless their good fortune and assume the worst. She has been struck down by an incurable disease, she is not long for this world. The women try not to look her in the eye, not to know too much. The teenagers do their best to ignore her. They are out of place anyway in such a theatre foyer, brought along by over-eager godparents or fissured-family obligation, forced here by tickets and purchases proving they are still unaware that while the child is no longer a child, he or she is also not ready for the step to adulthood that might make the Christmas treat again a joy. The quite young and still-young are not yet ready to process the fear that seeing another woman in pain stirs in them. She carries an obvious signifier of bodily decay but she is not that much older than them. Twenty years perhaps, and though those twenty years seem many more decades, even the most callow recognize her clothes are younger than their parents' dress, her hair is a better cut and colour. And yet she carries that stick. She is a symbol of death in their post-Christmas glitz and it is not right they should have to look at her. The teenage boy passes his friend another bottle of the illegally bought Bacardi Breezer with which his step-father hopes to ingratiate himself and they turn from the dangerous sight the stick-bearer offers. The limping woman is a witch to make them think of these things.

She continues her slow hop march through the room and now

there is a teenage girl looking at her. She looks like a teenage girl. That is, she looks with the manner of a teenage girl – half defiant stare, half embarrassed snigger. She cannot help herself, her face simply forms into the sneer of near-shame. Shame for the woman walking with a stick and shame at her own more than passing interest. This is the look that has not yet perfected itself into a mask of adulthood. It does not entirely understand how to lie, covers itself with squint and sneer and giggle and wide-eyed wonder that a body could do so much damage to its walker. Not that this girl does not fight her own bloody body battles, not that her own skin and flesh and not-enough-bone have not betrayed her often enough – but that a body should do so this publicly. The teenage girl endures agonies both silent and loud-voiced but despite her constant cries – or perhaps because of their very open nature – she is also perfectly aware that most of what makes her cry and lie awake at night is not all that obvious. She has read the books and seen the educational videos they provide at school, she may have anorexic body, but she does not have anorexic head. She is often in pain and at the same time she absolutely knows that in the eyes that look out of other heads, she is perfectly gorgeous and young and fine. There is nothing about her – even with the thin arms and legs – to suggest to the general public that she might be harmed. This girl lives in the real world after all, where a stick-thin teenage girl with jut-out cheekbones and shaded elbow sockets is more whole and less obvious than a not-quite middle aged woman walking with a dragon's head stick. The girl knows the pecking order here. She is not too shy to look.

People the stick-bearer's own age glance and take care. Their looks contain curiosity too. She should not be here perhaps. She does not have a small child on her arm, a whining teen at her back. Why has this woman come to this foyer alone, for whom is she waiting in obvious pain? Parents drag their heedless toddlers back from her wake, pull away little arms and stumpy legs that travel on with no regard, heads turned this way and that, eyes darting distracted from colour to sound and cannot see that which is directly in front of them. There are assumptions of car crashes and birth defects, cancerous disease and minor ailments. Perhaps this evening out is a last treat. Though the woman appears to have all her own hair – short hair but surely her own. She is not especially grey or wasted, fails to conform to the televisual anti-glamour picture of terminal illness. Maybe then, it is a simple breakage, something that will heal with time. Perhaps the stick she holds is the result of a night out and a fall into the gutter of drunken excess. But there is no certainty. And as long as the reason for the stick is unknown, the there-but-for-the-grace-of-God-ers are forced to offer her the benefit of the doubt. Yes, maybe the woman did cause this injury to herself. But then again, perhaps she was run over in a horrific hit-and-run accident, losing all her babies and possibility in one fell swoop. Perhaps she is dying slowly and painfully of one of the many degenerative diseases that acronym-swamp our present passing. Perhaps this is the last ballet for one who once danced herself. There are so many possibilities, and the stick which offers up each one confirms none. That being the case, the limping, leaning woman is given a wide berth and safe passage through the thronging crowd. A crowd that opens up to let her pass and then, when she has moved from immediate eye-contact space, turns to look after her, watch her go. They hold their breath and wait. She is ill somehow, they would rather she would go.

She can feel them look after her, knows the sensation, though she has usually been the starer not the stared at. Her grandmother had a stick. The old woman who, in her excessive age, rarely left her dark-furnished room except to shout at the little girl when she was playing the tuneless piano too loudly. The piano was for dance, not music. It was not there for itself, what it alone had to offer, it was an adjunct. Without feet and tempo and time steps the piano might as well be silent. The piano should be silent. At night the woman would climb up, high bedstead, candlewick bedspread, placing her stick carefully by the bedside table, its carved marble head leaning against her glass of water, her headache pills, her stomach pills, her back pills. The black head of a trusty Labrador pinned firmly into a rich maple branch, honed and sanded but with three intentional kinks left in to show its true origins, the Labrador's ears and sensitive snout worn silky smooth by her years of use. This cantankerous grandmother did not have her stick because she was an old woman. To the little girl it seemed an astonishing possibility, but she was not always an old woman. Sometimes it came in handy, now that the stairs were too much, when her rheumatic knee claimed attention, but she'd had this stick since she was just twenty-eight. Fit and healthy then in every way. Though she no longer uses it for its original purpose, she always used a stick for her work.

A dance teacher, she began with a cane and worked her way through several more before this model, old even then, was presented to her as a parting gift from a high-flying student. It is the stick that has pushed in a thousand backsides, turned out a million toes, beaten scores of repeated time steps into the dance hall floor. *Glissade*, *jeté*, *pas de chat*, *tournée*, *glissade*, *pas de bourrée*, but no, stop, not like that, and no! The piano stops, the weekday needle is dragged from the gramophone, the Saturday morning pianist reaches for her knitting, the class of girls pause, mid-step, breathless and flushed, sweaty streaks of hair sneaking from heavy-pinned buns. All wrong, you are all wrong! Turn out and right out and here and easy and hold and now – prepare and face and point. But not like that, not like that – like this girls, how many times must I show you? Do it like this. Like me. Like this. Watch me. And then the moment they wait for in every class comes and she lifts her long skirt so all the girls can see the suspenders and corset she wears, firming and framing her body into the straight sylph she was at nineteen when she too flew high and away only to land back home with a bump and the necessity of a small town teaching career. But they did not know that then. They only saw an older woman and her high stockings, ageing legs, veined thighs, the belly-button giggles catching them before the stick did.

Staying too-long weekends with her unwilling grandmother, the stick was the last thing the little girl saw when the old woman turned out the light and closed the box room door behind her, the first thing she heard in the morning when it began its nose-tap tap on the wall next door, its owner crying out for her cup of tea, the in-bed treat she claimed should be also be a treat for the grandchild. A treat to take care of her elderly relative, a privilege to be given the responsibility of the heavy black kettle, the gas fire, the porcelain cup and saucer, the heavy milk with cream floating in yellow globules across the surface of the jug. An honour then, to walk into that dark room where the curtains were never opened and the ivy had been allowed to grow over the French windows and the calendar stayed on the wall, the same faded picture of *Our Lady of Lourdes* and the exact date it had shown fifteen years ago when the old woman's husband died and the stick ceased its incessant poking at the recalcitrant turn-out of young girls, became instead the only thing left to lean on.

It was not a treat. It was a fearful journey every morning, wracked with the possibility of dead grandmothers and the looming photograph of the long-dead grandfather and the smell of denture fixative and the likelihood of spilt milk to sob over, stewed tea and cracked china. It was never a treat. But today's ballet is. Both for this younger woman and her partner. And so, despite the pain and the looks and with the help of the dragon's head stick, they will go out. Brave the crowds and the braying ballerina children, little girls in itchy princess dresses and pointy plastic tiaras, parents dressing up their dolls to remake the unfulfilling treats of their own childhood. Knowing it cannot work but trying anyway. Impossible to recreate the perfect turn-out but trying anyway.

Her partner taking too long in parking, she makes her way to the disabled toilet, pushing her stick out and across her body as she so often watched the grandmother do. The door is locked, a red engaged sign in a shiny new bolt. This place has recently received lottery funds, the money spent on toilet doors was surely a vital component of the budget application. She waits a minute, another five, the door opens, a mother and toddler walk out. The mother looks at her and before the face, the clothes, the woman before her, she immediately sees the stick. The stick glows in the dim corridor with a sense of entitlement and – in this queue only – privilege. The mother looks down at the toddler as if in explanation, excuse that will turn into defiance if necessary. The stick-bearer doesn't care in the least. But the mother does. And hurries her daughter away.

Finally a lift and several carefully negotiated steps later, she sits beside her partner in a specially arranged aisle seat and waits for the slow confection of the staged picture to begin. The stick-bearer has been far more ill than this. This is a minor physical disability. The burning ache, the throbbing waves are debilitating yes, but minor in that they will pass. Already in the past fortnight the extremes of pain have started to recede. She has been far more ill than this, with no hope of let-up or stick to clear her way. She has stood several times on the edge of insanity, her nails ripping from their tucked-up finger-beds as she tries to claw herself out of the falling pit. And she has fallen and stayed fallen and hidden in the dark and lost in the maze. But then she looked well enough on the outside. She is not one who shows her distress in weight loss or gain, tired eyes or red nose. And she did not have a stick. There was nothing physically wrong with her and no accommodation was ever made for the fact that from her more usual place of pain, this aisle seat would have been a torture, simply walking through that crowded foyer would have taken reserves of courage and fortitude impossible to measure. And even so, because the world demanded it, she has made those walks and sat in those seats and dug her nails deep into her thighs to stop herself from crying out when the hurting was so severe as to undo even the clamped-shut mouth. But those times there was no wand to wave the people around her into semi-fearful compliance. And just as she knows that this physical disability will pass, so too will the other return, the progression and pain inevitable. Knowing this, she has chosen to enjoy her outing with the stick, take advantage of the stature and space it offers, thrill to the helpful feet and pitying glances. There will be time enough for ignorance later.

The curtains part, her partner sits attentive and eager, the stage rises to the applause and a long-dead grandmother adjusts imperfect feet with a heavy stick. At home that evening the lovers dance sugar on to sour plums and remember there will be better nights. Just as there will certainly be worse.

image: david walters
<drw@thefreeflowstudio.co.uk>

D.J. Taylor
Passage Migrants

Come mid-August the light in Sheringham began to change. In the past it had hung in duck-egg blues and greys over the warm summer sand. Now it had turned gun-metal: cloudy even when there were no clouds. Morris watched it again that morning as he stood in the big, untidy room that looked out onto the beach, pulling a hand uncertainly over the three days of stubble on his chin. On the couch, a yard or two from the high windows, snug under blankets and Morris's old parka jacket, the girl from the Marine Ballroom slept soundly on, orange hair thrown back over a makeshift pillow of supermarket bags.

It was about half-past eight. Outside there were terns massed on the sandbar – two hundred of them at least, Morris calculated. Further out, beyond the upturned boats and the wreck of a giant sandcastle built three days before, gulls skirmished over the breakers. Once, at dusk on a day such as this, Morris had seen what he assumed was a purple heron rooting through driftwood in the shallows, but for some reason the hastily-palmed camera had realized only vague shapes of grey and cobalt, the bird itself gathered up and lost in shadow. Thinking of the heron made him remember the figure on the couch. Morris hadn't meant to come home with the girl from the Marine Ballroom. To find her there eight hours later, pinched face white against the black cushions, was to register a troubling shift in routine, like setting out along the coast path on the cliff to find it strewn with granite blocks from the sea defences.

Traipsing along the sea front on his way to get a paper – the door slammed sharply behind him by way of a hint – Morris watched the tern armies huddled against the breeze. In an hour or so they would head north to the flats at Cley or Brancaster. He walked back the way he had come, noting other routines that were undisturbed: fishermen hauling crab boats over the shale; an ice-cream van being restocked from a delivery truck; dog-walkers silhouetted against the shore line. Back at the flat he found the girl from the Marine Ballroom sitting at the big deal table wearing one of his old T-shirts and eating slices of unbuttered toast.

'This bread must be a week old' she said. 'Look, it's got green bits growing out of it.'

Her hair was redder than he'd thought, Morris realized – a kind of scarlet orange with magenta tints. Seeing it bobbing above the table-top nonplussed him. It was outside his range. There was a rucksack he hadn't noticed yet, half-open on the floor and spilling books and tissues out over the sandy hardboard.

'Nice place you've got here,' the girl went on, 'apart from the cafeteria.'

Morris reckoned she must be a year or two younger than himself – twenty-two maybe, or twenty-three. He lingered for a moment by the window, gently lashing the sill with the furled copy of the *Cromer Mercury*, meditating another hint.

'Where are you staying?'

'The Beeches. Out on the Holt road. I don't suppose you know how to get there?'

Morris nodded. Everyone in Sheringham knew about The Beeches. On Friday nights Range Rovers drove out from Norwich, Cambridge – even as far as London – dropping off gangs of moneyed teenagers at the gate. Two years ago there had been a scandal when a girl drowned in the swimming pool. Still rapping the sill with the newspaper, he gave directions. Beyond the window the sky threatened rain.

'I've to go to work,' he said, casting out the final hint.

'That's OK. I'll let myself out.'

Morris left her there among the mouldy bread-crusts, the stacked crockery and the copies of *Norfolk Bird Club Bulletin*. Looking up at the window a moment or two later, as the flock of terns swept northward over his head, he could see her moving beyond the glass: a ball of orange flame bleeding into the nondescript greys and fawns behind.

Down at the marina they were gearing up for the late-summer rush. Mr Silverton thought the season would last another fortnight. Then the schools would go back and the trippers start to disappear. Morris sold ice-cream, mended a catch that had come off the door of one of the fun-pool cubicles and retrieved a walkman that someone had dropped into the deep end. At the mid-morning break he and Doug, the other assistant, sat and smoked cigarettes on upturned crates in the yard, hunched against the tubs of chlorine and the rusty generator spares, while Mr Silverton came down from the upstairs office and took a turn on the front desk. Outside fine rain fell against the Perspex dividing wall and they could see the shapes of the holidaymakers clustered against the big overhanging sign that said SHERINGHAM'S NEWEST INDOOR AQUATIC EXPERIENCE.

Curiously, the girl – her name was Alice, he now remembered – was there again at lunchtime. From his eyrie above the soft drinks dispenser, where the wiring had begun to come away from the wall, he noticed her turning over the rubbish in the bargain swimwear trays that Mr Silverton bought in job lots on the back of Norwich market: nonchalantly, but with an undisguised sense of purpose. When she saw him she came over and stood by the dispenser, waiting for him to descend.

'Does it always rain like this? In this part of the world, I mean.'

Out of the corner of his eye he could see Doug regarding him sardonically from the desk. 'Pretty much.'

'Do you get a lunch break?'

'It's another half an hour.'

Waiting in the foyer, while he sold tickets to a cub pack superintended by two mountainous Akelas, she looked oddly out of place, Morris thought, like one of the birds you saw at the big reserves further up the coast: blown off course, not sure what the food was like or whether the natives were friendly. They had a ploughman's in one of the pubs along the front, in a small room hemmed in by fishing nets and ancient lobster shells. Alice was a student, taking a year out between degrees. Mostly she lived at her parents' house in London, but there was talk of Edinburgh, Exeter, places even further flung. There were other people from The Beeches in the pub: two girls in striped men's shirts and sunglasses and a boy carrying a copy of *A History of Western Philosophy*. At intervals their mobile phones went off, and they fished unselfconsciously in bags and pockets to answer them. Bored with the conversation, Morris stared out over the beach and its flotsam – marauding bands of children, an old man in an antique bathing dress tottering gamely towards the sea.

'There's a party on Wednesday at the house,' Alice said, when he got up to go. 'Why don't you come along?'

'I'll do that,' Morris said. Wednesday was the day he worked late.

Back at the marina he found Mr Silverton cross-legged on the floor beside the ice-cream cabinet, surrounded by a pile of melting choc-ices and sky-ray lollies, trying to mend an electrical fault. He was a plumpish, middle-aged man with thick, brindled hair like a badger, whom Morris and Doug had christened 'The Fatman'. 'There's a bloke in the foyer wants to know about a party booking for the Bank Holiday,' he said, without looking up, 'you'd better go and talk to him.' Heading off to reception, Morris found that Alice's pale, parched face, the flock of terns on the beach, had mysteriously coalesced in his head, so much so as to displace the other things that burned there.

The afternoon wore on. Mr Silverton finished repairing the ice-cream cabinet and went off to do errands in town.

'What happens here in winter?' Morris wondered over their tea-break.

Doug, who lived down the coast at Cromer, nodded at the imputation of local expertise. 'You ever been here in November Morrie boy? Half the shops shut down. Fatman takes six weeks in Torremolinos. Day a week maintenance for the likes of us, if we're lucky.'

Though we would never dream of interfering, Morris's sister Julie had written a couple of days before from her house in Slough, *Gary and I feel it is time you faced up to your responsibilities*. It all depended what your responsibilities were, Morris thought. He had a memory of walking through the front door in Slough a year before and Gary instantly asking him to wipe his feet. There was a fifty pence lying on the scuffed lino beneath the reception desk, and he picked it up and put it in the till.

'Soft bugger, you are' Doug said, without malice. Outside an ice cream van's klaxon rose like an air-raid warning over the silent streets.

Late-summer came. Waking up in the flat, Morris could feel the time slipping away, like sand from the high dunes falling out of his hands, down to the distant beach. Alice had left a paperback novel behind her on the couch: puzzling, unrecognisable spoor, about a group of girls sharing a flat in Bayswater. Morris examined it a couple of times before he handed it back. There was nothing in it that he could fasten on, still less any clue to Alice. In the evenings they went exploring the empty Norfolk back-lanes to Holt, Happisburgh and Burnham Market. Here there were unexpected surprises: two blind men playing chess in a café near Wells; an artist in a graveyard near Gresham busily transforming the church into a terrifying surrealist skyscraper; an older world, turned in on itself, inviolate. Julie wrote again, gossip and warnings jumbled together. The children were doing well at school. His mother was ill. There was a bed for him whenever he wanted it. On the Bank Holiday it rained for seven hours. Mr Silverton sat at the reception desk ostentatiously leafing his way through travel agents' brochures. Doug had disappeared, gone off to Norwich or working at Yarmouth funfair – nobody quite knew. Julie's letters lay face-up on the deal table, covered with beer can ring-pulls and postcards of Sheringham seafront. 'Do you ever write back?' Alice wondered, putting a pack of groceries down on the floor. She had taken to buying him things, Morris registered: bags of sugar; men's magazines; Mars Bars. There was a soft, proprietorial air to the way she moved round the flat.

'What are you doing at the weekend?' he asked, on a whim.

'Nothing.'

'There's somewhere we could go,' he explained, 'somewhere I haven't shown you.'

'OK,' Alice said. 'I like surprises.'

Morris could see that she was intrigued, that it was the right thing to have done.

'Next week,' Alice said, as they sped out on the coast road that Sunday, 'I shall have to be getting back. Really and truly.'

Morris nodded, hoping that this would absolve him from speech. There were teal flying alongside the car, a long line of them heading north to the Wash. The sanctuary at Titchwell was just as he remembered it: a pinewood shop selling bird books and pairs of binoculars, elderly men in waders and soft felt hats drinking coffee out of Thermos flasks in the yard. On the sheet of card tacked to the wall there were details of the passage migrants: stone curlews, avocets, an osprey that had flown in that morning with a Swedish ring tag round one of its claws. Later they wandered off along the path to the sea, past the twitchers' hides and the observation points. The light had gone grey again, Morris saw, turning the sky the colour of the filing cabinets in Mr Silverton's office.

'What was that?' Alice wondered, tugging suddenly at his sleeve. Morris felt rather than saw the blur of movement at his feet – like a brightly-coloured paper bag, he thought later, lofted skywards by the wind. Watching it come to rest, a dozen yards down the path, orange crest bobbing above the dark wings, he felt a surge of exhilaration.

'It's a hoopoe,' he said. 'Look! I never saw one before.'

There was a file of middle-aged women in mackintoshes coming along the path towards them. Boxed in, the hoopoe took flight again, westward over the salt marshes. Morris watched it go. Not long after it began to rain again and they retired to the car.

'That festival I was telling you about in Devon,' Alice said briskly, 'once I've parked my stuff in town I'm off down there. You ought to come.'

Morris stared through the streaming window as the bird-watchers' cars manoeuvred through the mud. The hoopoe would be somewhere over the north sea now, far away from the camcorders and the binocular arcs, out where he couldn't follow.

'Sorry,' he said, seeing the beach in winter, snow on the breakers, blanketing the rock pools in soft, white fur.

'Things to do.'

Rachel Bradford
More Chips and Scraps

Ugly Money

She gave him chocolate buttons to lie still under the bed. Counting pairs of used up knickers, silky, slippery, all the colours of the Test Card.

'In his pockets when his back's to the mirror. Good little magpie.'

All that paper, not pretty like Monopoly. Ugly money, dull as shit and Bovril. He could come out when he heard the feet go.

Sometimes, for the big notes, she'd kiss him on the head and smile. But only after she'd drawn her lips back on.

Nicely Turned Out

Nan moaned like a bastard all the way through Rock DJ.

'Well I like Holby City. Is this on every week, this Bints Awards?'

I sat on the arm of the settee watching her milky eyes, lilac lids so thin they might rip if she had to open them right wide. Fluttering about like dying butterflies behind big thick Diedre glasses that she wore for telly.

Coldplay gave her the heartburn she said, depressing she said, like beagles on valium. At least Ant and Dec were nicely turned out.

We had to go to be in bed before Eminem. 'S not fair. All me mates Nans are dead.

Cull

The Teletext had a page called Cull, in coloured writing at the bottom between holidays and entertainments. He'd watched the news at dinner and teatime but he still clicked on. More pyre pictures with the legs sticking up, Desperate Dan's barbeque stretching right across the field. They showed bar charts to compare with 1967, back in the days before Linda McCartney's.

They had to burn a lama in Essex.

A farmer had taken his own life, but they didn't say how. But he'd have to be buried anyway.

The Likes Of You

Police called it a crime of horrific and senseless brutality. They had no leads.

'I fought in the war for the likes of you.' That's what he would have told them, as they bound his wife's arthritic ankles to the scalding boiler pipes.

A carriage clock was all they got. Engraved, for forty-three years loyal service. And a gold bracelet, chock full of charms, too heavy to wear, it had sat in the jewellery box like a brace of fishing flies. It would have been their daughter's one day.

She couldn't give a clear description, she had cataracts.

And he died before the ambulance came. But not from fright, or from his heart. He choked to death on the piece of tongue he bit off when they smashed him on the head so hard with his own false leg that it cracked the roof of his mouth.

Rascal

My Uncle's kidneys packed in tea-time somewhere in between Wheel of Fortune and The Simpsons.

'Always on a Friday innit? Makes things so hard to sort out.'

He was famous in our family for being a rascal. They could spend a whole Boxing Day tea just talking about his women.

He never did take care of his blood sugar, he got gangrene and had maggots put in his leg to eat out the bad. They had to cut them off in the end, a good job his eyes went, he never could look at the stumps.

They'll have Welsh cakes back at the house after, and other things he wasn't allowed. No one'll pat their eyes and say he had a good run. They'll say he was a one, a stubborn old bugger. And you couldn't tell him nothing.

B.A.N.E.S.

The council changed their name again, from Avon like the lady, to Bath and North East Somerset.

Poor old girl, she jumped through all the hula hoops like a mongrel terrier in an embarrassing hat and collar. She had all the points: just one dependent and an asthma attack away from a full house.

They wrote such a lovely letter. They were so sorry, there was no room in the entire Inn, and the stable had been sold off for redevelopment. So fuck your luck, yours sincerely . . . ever such nice headed paper.

BANES. Rhymes with drains, chains and chilblains.

Appropriate Response

It was a second class stamp, but still, white envelopes were always welcome. I save them till last, to have with a roll up.

Sat on my feet till my legs go dead and the dog's drunk my tea.

He's got a whole language he learnt in therapy, all the sentences begin with I feel. No toss to argue. Wish I'd gone and learned that, but I had rent arrears and a fridge to defrost. The answer phone's unplugged, the mobile's run out.

I have to write in felt tip cos I dig too deep with a biro. Thank you for your honesty, I say. I'm having an appropriate response.

And the envelope glue tastes like foil and tinned potatoes, but it stops me screaming. Screaming till the ulcers in my mouth burn right off.

Why can't he just have his feelings indoors like everybody else?

image: will pearson
<will@digitaldreamworld.co.uk>

Nell Dunn

Penny and Marilyn

When I met Marilyn I had three lovers on the go. I was a very naughty girl. Later she told me, 'directly I set eyes on you I knew I was going to spend the rest of my life with you,' and she did.

We went on holiday to the South of France and you discovered we were near Vence and must see the Matisse chapel. I had never been touched by Matisse. We went in a taxi so as not to get lost. And here on the glass, through the glass, the coloured light swept by the sunlight into that small, simple space. Bathing us in blue and yellow ribbons of colour. There was such a sense of stillness we held our breath. After a few minutes you turned and said, 'Aren't you glad we came?'

I squeezed your hand.

In the hospital she made me her next of kin. She wanted me to be treated with the same respect as a husband or wife.

The operation took seven hours and afterwards the surgeon asked to speak to me. She explained it was more complicated then she thought, and that there had been a tumour the size of a melon in her womb and that it had grown through the womb onto the bladder and the kidney, and that there were probably cancer cells in the lining of the stomach.

They would know more when the results came back from the lab.

When Marilyn came round she had tubes coming out of everywhere. As I tried to make my way round the bed to get to her, it was difficult to manoeuvre so I put my hand on the drip, and it came to pieces and nearly fell apart on top of her, and she said, 'Oh fucking hell Penny!' because I'm always cack-handed. I managed to slot it back in and in spite of her agony we were both laughing.

Then she said, 'I know it's very serious and Pen, it's you and me.' 'Yes,' I said, 'we're in this together and we'll get through.'

Then the surgeon came, 'It's very, very serious,' she said, and told her everything.

I started to cry and she said, 'Pen, it's all right to cry.' I leant over the bed and we put our arms around each other and she faced up to it straight away.

All her love and thoughts were for me. She was the strong one.

'But you're my tower of strength,' she said.

Then the doctor came and told us that what Marilyn had was a carcinoma, a very rare one, and that it was the opposite of winning the lottery, which was a rather strange thing to say, but that's what he said. He said he would give her a real battering with platinum chemotherapy, she had to have six treatments of chemotherapy. The side effects are horrific, but it was her only chance of survival, there was no choice, while there is life there is hope.

I thought it would work.

After the first lot of chemo she came home and was in a lot of pain.

She was very poorly, very poorly indeed.

She had morphine patches and liquid morphine. She began to feel a little better and I had never cooked, she had always been the cook, but I began to cook all her favourite dishes. I became as good as Delia Smith and she put on eight pounds!

An enormous euphoria.

We listened to the Emperor Concerto and Barbara Streisand. We watched our French and Saunders videos and *The Life of Birds*.

Then the second chemo. And she became very ill.

What had happened was one of the nurses had put the wrong lead on the box and so instead of going through in twenty-four hours it had gone through in fifteen. It made her very ill. There was a big notice in the ward which read: NURSES PLEASE MAKE SURE YOU PUT THE RIGHT LEAD IN FOR GIVING CHEMOTHERAPY. THE WRONG LEAD CAN BE VERY DANGEROUS.

There weren't enough nurses. Patients were calling out for the nurse. They were in pain. She was in pain.

'Nurse, I'm in pain.'

I asked for a room of our own and I moved in and took care of her. We were there for two weeks. I did everything except give her the chemo.

She had to have a blood transfusion. It was meant to go in in four hours, instead the bag was empty in forty minutes. The clip that allows the flow had been incorrectly adjusted. The nurse apologized. The doctor said there was nothing more to be done.

She had a terrible pain in her back. She begged the doctor to re-examine her scan. He came back and said, 'I'm sorry, there is another tumour on the back of the pelvis, we didn't see it before because we weren't looking for it.'

But you get to a stage where it's no good being angry, you've got someone in pain and what can you do?

'You'll have to have radiotherapy on that one, the chemo won't touch it.'

As soon as she could walk with the drip she wanted to go home.

She can walk with a stick but she is losing weight rapidly. I can't tempt her to eat. The district nurses came. The Macmillan nurse came. They were all wonderful. Marilyn sat at her desk and booked a cruise for us in the spring. It was going to be the holiday of a lifetime. She said, 'If anything happens to me, Pen, take your Mum.'

I couldn't face the fact she was going to die.

She gets the lawyer round and she sorts out everything. All her affairs are in order.

At six o'clock on Christmas Eve she collapses on the floor. The doorbell goes and it's our doctor. 'Thank God you're here.' We get her into bed and he goes.

She began to vomit black, and got diarrhoea at the same time. It got worse and worse and worse. The district nurse came round, but then she went. And I was alone. I went down into the garden and screamed into the night. I screamed and screamed.

On the third night, after having been sick for three days and three nights, I rang the hospital. 'Keep her at home,' they said, 'See how she is tomorrow.'

I thought she was going to die. I rang the ambulance. We went to casualty. They gave her a drip. Marilyn said, 'Get your Mum.' My mother came to the hospital. I was crying.

Marilyn said to her, 'Penny has been wonderful, she has done everything for me.' My mother said, 'Thank you for making Penny so happy.'

She stayed in hospital for a week and then she came home again. A lovely community nurse came every day. He was called Neil and he was a mountaineer. The district nurse brought a water bed to make her more comfortable. She was so thin. She was in pain.

Marilyn wanted to die in a hospice. 'I don't want to die at home. I don't want to die in agony.'

We went to the hospice, and the doctor spent two hours with her.

'How do you feel?' I asked her.

'It' s wonderful to be here,' she said.

She was a very fastidious person, she liked clean things. The hospital wasn't clean enough. The hospice was spotless, and they looked after both of us. No more pain.

She couldn't live up to it. But she still had style. She liked making the nurses laugh.

On Sunday the doctor asked to speak to me. 'The cancer is everywhere, it's just a matter of time,' he said.

Even then, she was still breathing. I still didn't think it was going to happen.

She knew. She said, 'I've done everything, to look after you, Pen. You' re going to be all right and I want you to live for both of us. I want you to make every day special.'

She said, 'I don't mind if you meet someone half an hour after you bury me, I want you to be happy, Pen. Live for both of us. Enjoy life. You will never be without me. I shall be with you all the time.'

She couldn't protect me from her death. She wanted me to accept it. She said, 'Thank you for everything.'

She gave me strength. She said, 'This is it Pen, this is it. It's just you and me. No bullshit. Everything is clear. This is it.'

I felt totally loved.

I was frightened I wouldn't be able to live without her but I couldn't tell her that, because what could she do?

'I want you to be happy,' she said.

I said, 'I love you with all my heart, we were always meant to be together, always, always.'

I brought in pictures of her to show them how beautiful she was. She looked so poorly then. I wanted them to see what she really looked like.

She began to hallucinate figures round the bed. It was the morphine. 'It's OK darling,' I said, 'it' s the morphine that's doing it, there' s no one else in the room.'

In a few days she was more or less unconscious from the morphine. I was desperate. I called Sister Pauline, who was a friend of Marilyn. She came to the hospice.

'Can I say a prayer, Penny?'

I' d never met her.

'Marilyn was a very special person,' she said.

'I know,' I said.

I slept in a chair bed by her side.

They asked me if I'd like to see the chaplain. I was so desperate I said, 'Yes.' When he came he was wearing a rainbow badge and I realized they had got me a gay vicar.

At about three o' clock in the morning you came to and tried to talk. I couldn't make it out. You wanted me to go home . . . the postcards . . . you were desperately trying to find the right words . . . I finally understood . . . you were talking about the visit to the chapel at Venice. And that an Italian family who had visited the hospice the day before in tears, please bring in a postcard to comfort them . . .?

'The Matisse postcards?' I said.
A long sigh of relief. 'Yes,' she said. I dashed home to fetch them.

When she died there was a rainbow in the room.
There was no rush at the Hospice. I stayed with her a long time. I lay down on the bed next to her. I felt her love. Then my mother came and fetched me.
They came and took her corneas, that's what she'd wanted. I had a handwritten letter from Moorfields saying they had gone to two people, that meant a lot.

Before I met Marilyn I'd had a lot of love affairs. I had three on the go when we met. But after I met Marilyn I only wanted her.

I went to Fortnum and Mason to buy the wine for her funeral. You see she was a very stylish woman, was Marilyn.

Sarah Wood

NOTHING IS SERIOUS

Close-up on a hand spinning a football-sized inflatable globe on the end of one finger. The world spins faster and faster, then another hand stops the ball, both hands weigh up the globe for a moment then throw it away.

Black and title : **NOTHING IS SERIOUS**

INT: Early morning, dark, bedroom.

A galaxy of stars fills the screen, some near, some far, catching the light. Faintly in the distance, then louder as the camera moves across the skies, voices –

DJ RADIO VOICES

Let's count it down. (Sound of cheering) It's not seven, it's not six, it's not five. It's just four days to go. (More cheers) Are you ready? (Mock sincere) Can you put your hand on your heart and say you're ready? Because remember. He sees you when you're sleeping. He knows when you're awake. He knows if you've been bad or good . . .

Santa Claus is Coming to Town starts playing brashly.

During the dialogue one of the stars falls and the camera follows its descent as it lands on EMILY lying in bed. The galaxy we have

been crossing is stick-on fluorescent star shapes, not heaven at all, simply part of a teenage bedroom.

EMILY
(picking the star off her cheek and looking at it)
Hmph.

She stands on the bed, sticks the star back up, sits down again pulling the covers back round her shoulders. She pulls the clock radio round so she can see the time (7.30). Lies back down, stares blankly up at the stars, listening to the Christmas song on the radio. Changes her mind, gets out of bed.

INT: Early morning, light, kitchen and interior of house.

Dressed, lit by the morning light coming in the window and with the sound of daytime TV excitably noisy in the background, she looks in the fridge.

We see inside from her point of view. There's nothing much in it, just some half-opened packets.

At the sink, EMILY stares out of the window.

She looks at the view of a winter back garden.

She eats some cereal out of a bowl which she then carries with her as she walks through the house drawing the downstairs curtains, picking up the mail, opening it blankly in front of breakfast TV –

TV ANNOUNCER (unseen, shouting at each other)
Why are you being so serious? Nothing's that serious at this time of the year. It's Christmas! Stop being so serious! Get some Christmas spirit why don't you!

Music over, and the tone changes as a new voice takes over from the last.

SECOND TV ANNOUNCER

Well, it's at this time of year though that we have to spare a thought for those who are alone. So we visited a children's home in south London to see just what a bit of cheering up can do. (Sounds of children shouting.)

EMILY flicks off TV with remote control, turns, taps the side of a lighted tropical fish tank.

The fish dart away from her.

INT: Early morning, light, upstairs.

Back upstairs, now dressed, EMILY draws her bedroom curtains, lets the light in, makes her bed, packs up her bag, turns off the radio, checks herself in the mirror.

At the top of the stairs, just as she's about to go downstairs, dressed for outside, she pauses on the landing outside another bedroom.

She hesitates, looks ahead of herself, then glances down, checking herself, momentarily sad.

We see from her point of view the drop of the stairs as they curl out of sight.

EXT: Morning, light, on a bus.

EMILY is squashed in an inside upstairs seat by a girl who is talking loudly but apparently incidentally to a woman across the aisle.

WOMAN

Did you watch it? We'd never seen it before. The boy has to keep these two stupid burglars out of his house because his family have forgotten him. Mind you he gives as good as he gets.

GIRL
Oh, that. *Home Alone*?

The WOMAN nods yes enthusiastically.

GIRL
We've seen it hundreds of times.

EMILY sits all the time looking out of the window.

We see from her point of view, through the distorting, sticky finger-marked window next to her, the suburban roads, the houses, and as the bus slows, a flock of crows flying up as the bus passes the gates to a large green cemetery.

EMILY looks down until the bus has moved past the cemetery. She pretends to look for something in her bag. But as the bus moves off, she casually watches the birds disappear out of sight beyond the top corner of the window.

INT: Fluorescent light, shopping centre.

Generic shopping centre sculpted birds hang from a glass ceiling. Camera tips down from the birds' height to an overhead shot of EMILY dressed as a Santa's elfin helper outside a grotto in the middle of the concourse. She's holding back a small queue of children.

EMILY
OK. Next one, just go in and tell Father Christmas what you want.

A SMALL GIRL WITH HER HOOD UP walks forward and disappears inside holding her Christmas list proudly in front of her.

EMILY (to two GIRL SISTERS behind)
Just write on this piece of paper what you want from Father Christmas.

EMILY glances round.

A second SANTA HELPER waves at her through the curtained door to the grotto.

EMILY
OK. Next.

The GIRL SISTERS look at her indignantly. They haven't even started writing their lists.

EMILY
Just go in and tell Father Christmas what you want.

She stands straight, stretches her back and looks round for more children despondently.

MAN PASSING
Cheer up, it might never happen.

The MAN PASSING walks on, sniggering to his GIRLFRIEND. They both turn and look at EMILY and walk on.

She looks after them. She sweeps up some dropped sweet papers and Christmas lists with a child's size broom. She picks out one of the lists and reads it. Crumples it and throws it in a bin with the rest.

SANTA HELPER appears.

SANTA HELPER
You do leading out for a bit. It's cold out here.

EMILY
You mean it's weird in there with him.

SANTA HELPER
Fair's fair.

EMILY disappears inside. In the grotto, 'Walking in the Air' from *The Snowman* is playing tinnily on a loop.

SANTA
Bit of a lull.

EMILY
Lunchtime. Everyone's in McDonalds.

SANTA
(fixing his beard into place, nodding towards the entrance)
Spoke too soon.

A VERY SMALL GIRL appears, gives SANTA her list, looks afraid like she's going to cry.

SANTA looks nervously at EMILY.

EMILY quickly tries to gives the VERY SMALL GIRL an inflatable world.

EMILY
Don't worry. Your mother's waiting just outside the door.

The VERY SMALL GIRL looks like she's going to make a bolt for it.

EMILY
Here, let me take your Christmas list for Santa.

She takes it and hands it to him.

SANTA
Oh, thank you. Now have you been a good little girl?

The VERY SMALL GIRL looks frightened again.

EMILY shakes her head at him to stop his act.

EMILY

There, I bet you're very good. Take it (holding out the ball). This is your free gift from Santa.

SANTA (hopefully)

Happy Christmas and I'll see what I can do with this list.

EMILY leads the VERY SMALL GIRL down a short red nylon tunnel back to the outside world.

As they emerge we see the shopping centre from her P.O.V. and for a split second, in a frozen moment, she sees the MOTHER waiting for the VERY SMALL GIRL as her own, smiling at her, waiting for her to come back from the grotto. She straightens up still held by the vision and only snaps out of it as the VERY SMALL GIRL loosens her grip and runs to her waiting MOTHER, dropping the inflatable globe so that it rolls slowly round the back of the grotto.

EMILY shakes her head to clear the image of the waiting mother and goes to retrieve the globe.

CLOSE-UP of the globe in her hand as she spins it and drops it back into a box with hundreds of others.

Soundtrack of the slightly distorted, tinny 'Walking in the Air' comes up over shopping centre noise heralding –

A collage of images of EMILY as the same thing happens time after time – the moment when she emerges into the shopping centre with a child and a new family group reforms in front of her eyes, each time a mother stepping forward to collect a child.

Eventually it gets too much, she calls back through that she's going on a break.

She walks through the centre, obvious in her elf costume, oblivious to the comments of people walking past.

The only highlighted moment is when passing a hairdressers a NEWLY PERMED LADY is leaving, self-consciously, lightly fingering the shape of her new hair, a little embarrassed, wanting the glamour and the newness of it away.

As EMILY passes she overhears a scruffy girl windowcleaner – GINA – who is cleaning the big square panes of the hairdressers' windows.

GINA
Looks nice.

NEWLY PERMED LADY (shyly)
Oh. Thank you.

From EMILY's P.O.V. we can see the NEWLY PERMED LADY walking away happier, relaxed.

EMILY glances back at GINA but she's obliviously soaping the glass. Behind EMILY, the final scene from *It's A Wonderful Life* is playing in all the TV's in a shop window.

INT: Shopping centre, staff room.

In a small cramped staff room of mixed staff from different shops EMILY is sitting with a heavily made-up lady from a department store Lancôme counter.

LANCÔME LADY
It's nice you're seeing your sister for Christmas.

EMILY
Yeah.

LANCÔME LADY
It'll be a hard one. The first one's always hard. Are you staying in your – (she pauses) in the house?

EMILY
No. She's driving up on Christmas Eve and we're both going down to her boyfriend's parents in the New Forest.

LANCÔME LADY (kindly)
Well, just bear in mind, the first year's always the worst. If you can get through this one, I promise you, you'll never feel it as bad again.

Some SHOP BOYS come in noisily. EMILY looks embarrassed, talks quieter.

EMILY
What are you doing for it?

LANCÔME LADY
Same as usual.

LANCÔME LADY gets up, keeps talking but starts washing out her coffee mug. There's a line of lipstick round its rim where her mouth's been.

LANCÔME LADY
It's the new year I hate. Last year we went to sleep and set the alarm to wake us up at midnight. Seems pointless really.

The SHOP BOYS snigger amongst themselves.

LANCÔME LADY (oblivious)
But one thing to think about, I mean, when you've had a rough year like you've just had, is to look on the bright side. It must still make you proud, Emily. Just thinking about all those GCSEs you got.

EMILY looks embarrassed.

LANCÔME LADY
Even though she can't, you know, know about it. Your

mother would have been so proud of you. Despite everything, you did that.

EMILY (really quietly)
She does know.

LANCÔME LADY
I mean, if our Jacqueline got half as many as you I'd be walking on air. Well, that's my time up. Send my best to your sister, she's a bright one too.

LANCÔME LADY leaves, EMILY sips at her tea, watches the sniggery SHOP BOYS who are poring over a cheap women's magazine.

FIRST BOY
Look at the size of her. Before *and* after you'd need a rope to climb on.

SECOND BOY
(sarcastic, looking at EMILY to impress her)
How'd you know?

FIRST BOY (oblivious)
That's disgusting. I'd rather die.

SECOND BOY (to EMILY)
Love signs – (reading article). Who's sleeping with who in the new Millennium. (To EMILY) What sign are you? (Fake spiritual) Let me guess, earth or air sign?

EMILY
(trying to finish her tea but it's too hot)
Don't know.

FIRST BOY
Don't be like that. Virgo, is it?

SECOND BOY
Don't get a face on, we're only having a laugh.

EMILY gets out a cigarette, starts to light it.

SECOND BOY
I wouldn't do that. It's not very 'elfy.

They both laugh out loud. EMILY looks down at her costume, puts her cigarette back in its box.

EMILY
Think I'll go and smoke this outside.

SECOND BOY
Want us to come too?

FIRST BOY
Shut up will you, I'm still trying to guess. Come on give us a clue, is it scorpio? I'm scorpio.

EMILY pours her tea away and washes her cup quickly.

SECOND BOY (saucily)
Earth sign? Air sign?

FIRST BOY
(ignoring him, now quite interested in EMILY)
Earth, air, what is it, fire or water?

EMILY (stalking out)
Up in the air sign.

SECOND BOY
Stuck up, more like.

FIRST BOY
Not very friendly.

Another GIRL walks in.

FIRST BOY (nudging his friend)
Excuse me. My friend wants to know, what sign are you? Earth, air, fire or water?

SECOND BOY
Truth or dare?

FIRST BOY
Animal or vegetable?

INT : Shopping centre, lifts.

EMILY steps into an all-glass lift.

The ground pulls away dramatically as the doors close and it flies up fast.

EXT : Roof of the shopping centre. Wintry afternoon light.

On the roof of the building EMILY is toeing the edge of the flat roof miserably. She looks up at the sky, watches a flock of birds fly up from an opposite building, looks out over the grey city.

She smokes the last of her cigarettes, throws the butt and then the packet over the edge and watches them fall the several floors to the ground.

Suddenly from behind her a voice. She turns –

GINA
Hello.

EMILY (guilty)
Oh. I was just smoking, you're not allowed downstairs.

She picks up her bag to go.

GINA
I like it up here too. I always save it until last.

EMILY
Save what?

GINA
Do you want a go? (She signals to the harness she's wearing) There's nothing like it.

EMILY
What?

GINA
Come and see for yourself.

She leads EMILY over to the other side of the building and shows her a harness and a platform on ropes attached to a pulley system.

GINA
Ever want to be in the movies?

She starts putting a harness on EMILY. Momentarily, like a child, EMILY lets GINA put it over her head and doesn't really realize until it's tied under her arms.

EMILY
No thanks.

GINA
(fixing a belt round her own middle)
Trust me. It'll make your Christmas. Something to tell the family.

EMILY looks pained.

GINA

There's nothing to worry about. I do it all the time. By myself. (EMILY shifts, scared, as she looks over the edge again) Nothing to worry about. I'll be holding on. And I'm the expert.

She smiles at her charmingly, holding out the last rope to be attached.

EMILY

I don't like the way you keep saying there's nothing to worry about.

GINA

(fixing the rope to EMILY 's harness)

There isn't. Just let go. (She edges EMILY to the very edge, gets her to swing her legs over the side) OK. When the rope goes slack, you move down. (Glancing over her shoulder quickly) Come on, get started. Or someone'll catch us.

Cut to shot of EMILY the elf hanging about five feet from the top of the building, frozen.

CLOSE-UP of EMILY, eyes tight shut, sweating, nervous.

EMILY

I don't think I . . .

From EMILY 's P.O.V., GINA's head appears, peeking over the edge of the building.

GINA

Just go.

EMILY takes a deep breath, pushes herself off the side and falls the first small distance. She holds still, looks up.

GINA appears above again.

GINA
Just let the rope out little by little.

EMILY starts feeding the rope through her hand slowly; slowly she descends, her eyes closed, praying under her breath.

GINA (unseen)
Very good. Just keep going.

EMILY descends about half the height of the building until she opens her eyes and sees the ground below again, the steep fall beneath her, and freezes.

EMILY
(Whispering to the wall in front of her)
I can't. I can't move.

GINA (unseen)
What's the problem? Just let the rope out gently.

EMILY looks down. A small crowd has gathered below and people are looking up, pointing. She closes her eyes, breathes deeply, tries to move, can't.

EMILY (to herself, praying)
Please – let – this – stop.

She slips some rope through her hand without thinking and sinks a few feet by mistake, surprising herself.

The crowd below *oohs* and *aahs*.

EMILY
Oh fuck.

GINA (calling down)
That's right. Just let the rope slide through your hands gently.

We see her from the P.O.V. of the people on the ground. She's hanging in the middle of the brightly-lit letters spelling out what Christmas films are playing - their titles, times and certifications illuminated round her. She's stuck in the air, right by where it says HAPPY CHRISTMAS FROM US ALL AT CINEMA CITY.

In CLOSE-UP again, EMILY shuts her eyes and the sound of the city below and the wind are heightened. She begins to shake a little and from somewhere very deep inside her she begins to call –

EMILY
Help. He – lp.

The crowd below are quiet, watching, but as they make out her help cry they start shouting instructions.

FIRST CROWD PERSON
Just come down slowly, you're nearly there.

SECOND CROWD PERSON
Don't give up now.

FIRST CROWD PERSON
Just let the rope out slowly.

THIRD CROWD PERSON
Not very far to go now, darling.

FIRST CROWD PERSON
Come on, you can do it

CROWD (falteringly together)
Come on. We're here. Come on.

EMILY opens her eyes a crack. She looks down, all the people wave. She looks up and can just make out GINA over the top, shouting instructions she can't hear anymore.

EMILY (to herself)
Okay Emily. Don't let it beat you. It's not far to go. It's not far to go. You can do it.

Cut to flashback of EMILY as a small girl on a bike with her mother holding on to the parcel tray at the back, steadying her as she tries to balance to learn to ride it. MOTHER is running up and down the garden behind the bike, shouting 'I'm holding on, I'm holding on,' as child EMILY cycles with great concentration. MOTHER goes inside to answer a ringing phone, and we see child EMILY set off again, summoning courage, convincing herself she'll be okay balancing by herself for the first time. She tells herself, 'She's holding on, she's holding on,' as she pushes off and starts cycling.

Back in real time, EMILY begins to let herself down the building. Falteringly, the crowd keeps shouting as she inches her way to them, they get louder and louder until a small cheer goes up as she finally comes down to the ground. They all surround her and laugh and hug her.

EMILY (laughs, bursts into tears)
Bloody Christmas miracle.

Everyone crowds round her smiling and congratulatory.

INT: Bus, evening light.

Cut to bus journey home, EMILY thinking, watching the evening city flash by outside. She sits back, relaxes.

INT: House, night time.

EMILY goes round the house putting on all the lights. She puts on the TV, flicks through the channels and finds *Meet Me in St Louis*.

She watches for a moment, then walks through the house again, the sound of the film playing in the background.

She climbs the stairs, stands outside the door she didn't go into in the morning. She pauses, thinks for a moment, takes a deep breath, then pushes it open and switches on the light.

Shot of the room from EMILY's P.O.V., the master bedroom, neatly made up but almost too neat, impersonal.

EMILY steps inside, glances round the room and we follow her gaze across the neat line of shoes, the dressing gown on the back of the door, the things on the dressing table, pill bottles on the bedside cabinet.

She takes another breath, walks across the room and looks out of the window. In the background, Judy Garland is singing 'Have Yourself a Merry Little Christmas.' She listens to it, emotion gathering in her face. She watches the view out of the window, what she can see in the dark.

We see the view from her point of view, the same garden path which we saw earlier in the flashback, several years on, wintery now.

She pushes open the window and flinches at the cold coming in. The curtains stir and the noise of the outside world, of traffic and air and people and dogs floods in.

She breathes in the new air, pauses, then turns, leaves the window open, takes in the room once more, smoothes the corner of the bedspread gently and then leaves the room, switching off the light.

The camera stays in the room, watching its stillness, only the curtains moving, and lit only by the external light of streetlights.

The soundtrack comes up of the final chorus of Judy Garland singing 'Have Yourself a Merry Little Christmas', and credits.

FINISH

Donald Paterson
Taxonomy

'What's the difference between azaleas and rhododendrons?'

The question goes round and round my head. What *is* the difference? Loch Maree stretches out ahead and the road twists down, its passing places heavy with civility. It's sunny. I shake my head. You ask, 'Is it to do with the size of the plant?'

'No, I don't think so.'

I can glance at you while I drive. I'd like to have the answer – to be able to say something knowledgeable like, 'The azalea has five petals and the rhododendron only four.' But I don't know the truth and we drive on, stopping and starting for the Shearings buses with their garish orange and blue paint, full of old startled faces. The question circles my mind.

'Maybe it's something to do with the kind of leaves. We'll look when we're there. I don't know, really.'

You seem satisfied by that and turn your face to the mountains, the grey mass of Ben Eighe with its scree pouring down. The sun's on your face so I don't mention the noise I hear from the engine. I couldn't describe it anyway, I don't think – it's just a noise that doesn't quite sound right. I would know if it wasn't there, but I don't think I can say exactly what it is or where it's coming from. I turn up the volume on the cassette player so that Mozart joins the sunshine in the car. I don't want to break down here, with a hundred and twenty miles or whatever to get back home. More, because we're not even half way through the journey yet. Maybe I should have asked you to take your car.

'Maybe it's something to do with the size of *flower*. I don't know really.'

You turn and smile. 'We'll look when we're there,' you say. I'd like to know. Once I know I'll not forget, I promise.

The thing is when you do look at them you can't tell the difference. Or you think you can but when you look at the label in the garden centre what you thought was an azalea turns out to be a rhododendron. Or the other way round, of course. But then, whoever puts the labels on must know.

I think this is a difficulty I have, that I've always had. I like to know what's what and why. I think that's human. And so must you or you wouldn't have asked. But when you're asking me, I wonder what happens when I can't give an answer? What effect would that have? But I can't ask that question because that's the one I *don't* want to know the answer for.

Slioch, over the water, glistens. A cormorant (I think) flies fast and hard above the surface, then it's hidden by trees. We had a coffee a while back in a hotel I don't remember the name of, served by an Australian waitress who'd just split up with her boyfriend. Split up *from* her boyfriend. She was wearing a tartan skirt. You had shortbread and I just had coffee. (I could do with another.)

Soon, we're driving through Gairloch and then Poolewe, white buildings and old cars, the smell of seaweed and a collie barking at the car as we pass with the windows down. I ask you if you're hungry.

'I don't mind,' you say. 'Are you?'

'Are you?' I say.

We park the car in the car park at Inverewe Gardens and walk to the restaurant and I tell you a story about something that happened there several years ago, before I knew you, which is a strange thing. The restaurant itself turns out to be a lot bigger and a lot emptier than I'd expected. The toilets are clean and one wall in the restaurant has a kind of mural on it. We queue and I choose a sandwich with cheese and tomato and a coffee and you have a coffee and the macaroni cheese with no side salad or chips or anything like that.

When we're sitting down, you're studying the printout from the till.

'Why was that so cheap?' you ask.

I study the printout.

You say, 'They've only charged me one pound for the macaroni. That can't be right.'

So you go back up to the till and try to negotiate an increase in the bill. While you're there I wonder if I would have done that, and I can't decide. But I'm right glad that you have. I like watching you try to pay more than you've been charged. The carnation and little bit of greenery on the table are plastic, which seems odd at Inverewe Gardens. When you come back over you tell me that they won't take any more money and you got a reduction because you didn't have a side salad or chips.

So after a few minutes I think I have a solution for this, which is that on the till there are only a certain number of little keys and each key corresponds to an item on the menu such as, say, macaroni with side salad and chips, but there's no key corresponding to macaroni on its own so therefore you can't be charged for that and the woman has to press a key for *something* on its own and the only thing she has on the key pad that is anything like would be the key that says 'side salad' or 'chips' and that's what really costs one pound and so that's what you've been charged for.

You seem happy enough with that.

After eating we go out and start our walk round the garden. First, though, in the entrance building, we look at the books for a while and pay for our tickets. Actually you pay for the tickets, laughing at me because we'd agreed this earlier and I'd forgotten and I feel so *good* about this that I foolishly buy a raffle book for a Scottish National Trust prize draw with a first prize of a trip to Rome and that's where we're going in the summer anyway.

The azalea and the rhododendron thing becomes a problem straight away as we walk up the drive. There are plenty other plants to look at too, but, what with it being May, we're really just here to see the rhododendrons and azaleas. Every bush, or tree or whatever, has a little label thing attached made out of some kind of metal, lead maybe. This label will tell you what kind of plant you're looking at, using two Latin words such as *Rhododendron Ciliatum* or whatever. I decide that the best way forward here (as we branch away up the slope away from the big house and towards Rhododendron Walk) is to *guess* each one by looking at it and then checking with the label.

We lean together in front of one with gaudy pink flowers and I say, 'Rhododendron.'

You say, 'Why?'

I say, 'I don't know but you've got to start somewhere.' And here it *is* a rhododendron, so I look at it a bit longer, taking in things like leaf shape, size of flower and so on. We spend a bit of time looking at a very odd kind of euphorbia that has little eyes looking at you. Then we look at another bush, this time with pale yellow flowers, and I guess rhododendron and *I'm right again*.

I'm so pleased that I can do this now and I talk fast, explaining to you how I've arrived at these two decisions and you nod as I explain about the waxiness of the petals and the arrangements of the leaves on the twigs. We walk on through the tall paths, blossom at our feet, and I get the next four wrong, then one right, then another two wrong. You laugh as much when I get it right as when I get it wrong.

'It doesn't matter,' you say, with your hand on my arm.

'It does!'

That's all. I can't explain why it *does* matter so much that I can get this right for you. I know fine that if I get it wrong you're not going to go away from me, but still I feel a lurch in my heart when that happens. This is stupid. I know fine. I find it hard to put into words, which is stupid too, since talking is what I'm good at. Depends what about, maybe. Anyway, it's funny, because they *all* seem to be rhododendrons, according to the labels. You take a photo of one, waiting quite a long time while some people move slowly out of the way.

There's a little bay at Inverewe Gardens so we go down the paths at the end of the peninsula and go there and sit on the bench looking out at the Camas Glas. It's as still as anything and the dark tide is out, so the front is covered with yellowy seaweed and a few bits of bleached wood. There's a thrush flicking its way through the weed, looking for little insects, and a chaffinch lands closer to us and both birds scavenge away. After each hop, the thrush looks at us, twenty feet off, and assesses how risky we are. The chaffinch does not seem to mind us so much. They seem to be different like that. I fight down the wish to talk about this. I don't need to talk here.

When we stand up to move on, the birds fly away, but once we are fifty yards up the path I look back and they've both returned or at least two other birds very like them have.

'Shall we go out to the point?' you ask.

'Fine.'

There's a kind of jetty thing with a bright red lifebelt hanging on a wooden board held to a post with leaking rusty bolts. Beyond that the land meets the sea in a black rocky outcrop. I clamber over the rocks and sit as far out as I can. There's thrift (*Armeria Maritima*) growing where it can in the cracks in the rock. I like it here. I scan the water. I don't know why, but I think there will be some seals appearing while I sit here, so I watch attentively for them. You're sitting further back, nervous I think of slipping on the weedy rock. So there we are, the water, then me, then you behind me, the little clumps of thrift in between. No seals come, but I like this arrangement. There is not much breeze and I turn back and see you wave your hand from not far away and for a moment I think it's a little wave at me and then you do it again and I realize that it's midges bothering you. I realise this just in time not to make a fool of myself by waving back. And, yes, I know that doesn't really matter much either.

It's just that when things seem right, how little we have to do to send the balance out. How easy to do wrong. How much we do not know and do not understand and so how much we risk every time we open our mouths or move or do *anything*. I mean I know you, very well, and I know so much of how you move and speak and still there's one thing I don't know, which is this: is there something which might change all that? I can think of a huge rock balanced on top of a hill. It will sit stable enough, but one day, as you have done every day for a hundred years, you climb the hill and sit down and lean against the rock and something's different. Your shoulder is not quite just so and you're touching another part of the rock with it. And let's say a rabbit races out across the grass in front of you and your heart beats harder for a moment there than it has for a hundred years and the tiny pulse goes through you into the rock, making it fall, crashing, through the trees below. What then?

So you see I don't know you at all. And that's what it is about the azaleas and the rhododendrons.

But anyway, we carry on up the paths and come to the

viewpoint overlooking the big bay. On the far side, at Inverasdale, some lorries are moving and the sound echoes loud across the water. Two little power boats head off from a jetty towards the fish farm further out to sea and the white foam spreads out behind them and then vanishes. There's a bench up there. It is dedicated with a metal plaque – brass – to two young people who were born together and died together some years ago. I can't remember the details now. We sit down.

'Maybe two twins,' I say after a bit. 'The children of the owner of the big house. Killed in a boating tragedy in Loch Ewe.'

Then I try a daring thing. It starts with me wondering what I sound like, saying such things. Do I sound stupid, I mean, always coming up with these explanations? So I think, what would it be like to be you, sitting here on my left, listening. I imagine myself *as you*, wearing the blue fleece and dark jeans. If I were you I'd feel my hair whipping lightly at my cheek. I'd feel smaller, turning up to my right to glance at me. I'd feel the hard pressure of the bench as my left arm lies along it as you lean that way into the wood. I feel the pressure of my right leg against my left as you sit cross-legged. I'm in behind your eyes watching out across the water. I manage this for a tiny second and it leaves my heart racing, for one moment when I'm not just clear in my mind who's who. Just for a moment. This is the best part of the day so far but it does not last long enough for me to find an answer to the questions that move in *my* mind.

Then we move on, you talking of your higher class and how they'll do in their exams: each child waiting for results which will send them on their own radius away from home. Every one waiting for the same thing so that they can later on be different.

We walk along the dry paths. I like the lungwort (*Pulmonaria Vulgaris*) and you like the Olearia (*Olearia macrodonta*). We come to something which we don't understand. There's a rhododendron that's grown up with two trunks, if that's the right word, the separation only about a foot above the ground. At about eye level a branch has grown out of the smooth wood towards the other trunk and, impossibly, joined it. The whole arrangement (if you ignore the other branches and the whole flowering top of the tree) forms an upside down letter A as the trunks diverge. Which trunk did the branch grow out of? Which trunk did the branch join? We cannot tell. We cannot tell how this can have happened. I wonder what name could be given to this arrangement and cannot come up with anything. We look at this for a while, running our hands over the smooth joins as the branch connects the trunks, getting no clues.

Clues or no clues, for some reason that neither of us can put our finger on, this is a beautiful thing to find in the garden, a perfect thing in its malformation. It seems we want to look at it for a long time, the lack of an explanation holding us still, and calm.

Then we're interrupted by someone – an elderly man with a red checked shirt and a fawn jacket, half-zipped. He's walking towards us down the path, taking small old-man's steps, his eyes ahead, staring.

'Excuse me,' he says, from twenty feet away, and he's American. 'Excuse me, folks,' he says.

We turn fully to him, smiling, still thinking of the rhododendron (or azalea) we've been studying. He trots slowly to us, just a little out of breath, his glasses a bit squint, his hands clutching at the hem of his anorak. We wait while he organises himself to speak. He is about seventy, I think, more or less twice my age.

'Say, have you people got a map about you?'

You start to take our brochure from your fleece pocket, and a yellow paper tissue comes out too, and as you stoop to lift it, he continues, 'I can't find Sarah. I've been roaming around hereabouts for a half hour.'

He is sort of laughing, making a joke of it but there is an edge to his voice, as if being without Sarah is an uncomfortable thing. His nervous hands give him away. As you flick through the leaflet, finding the centre pages with their diagram of the gardens, he goes on:

'Maybe if I could find the big house again. You think she might be waiting there? You think so?' His voice is still breathless.

We try to reassure him with the map, holding it in close between the three of us, pointing to features. Of course she'd be there, at Inverewe House, or maybe in the Visitor Centre, or in the restaurant, and certainly he should go to one of these places and just wait, because if they *both* keep moving they might be wandering, not meeting, for ages. I say to him that it's better to stay still than to be searching around. He accepts this, or seems to, and indeed it strikes me as a good thing to say, too, so I try a bit of light-heartedness to cheer him along.

'You could be lost for years in these gardens.'

He looks at me and says, seriously, 'Do either of you have any water to keep me going?'

'No,' I say, shaking my head apologetically. 'Sorry, we don't . . .'

As I say it I realize that in fact he wasn't meaning it. I think that at about the same moment he realises that I've taken him seriously when he has been trying, by making a joke, to reassure us that he's all right, since we've clearly been worried about him. I'm thinking that his comment is an American one: the dry prairies, the tumbleweed blowing past columns of Arizona stone, the thirst. I missed his meaning, I'm thinking, because I'm Scottish and it rains a lot here. And he's feeling bad now because he can see that he's embarrassed *me*, so I feel it's a shame for *him*. His wife would have understood his comment, but she's not here and suddenly the world is too huge for me.

For a second (maybe not that long) we're looking at each other and my heart is filling with a kind of sadness for him and for me, too. He looks much more lost than he was a moment before and now I feel it as well. Then you say:

'Look at this tree here. What do you make of this?'

Glad to be able to break this nearly intolerable moment, we both look at the tree and we talk for a few moments more about it. He can't explain it either and, given what's happened, it seems a bad way to part, so I ask him about the whole rhododendron and azalea thing that's been bothering me and to my surprise he knows the answer.

'An azalea's a kind of rhododendron,' he says.

'As simple as that?' you say, and I can't quite tell if you're pleased or disappointed, or which I am.

'Simple as that. The azalea belongs to the rhododendron genus,' he goes on. 'And the rhododendron belongs to the family *Ericaceae*.'

'Meaning?' I ask.

'*Ericas* are heathers. Like your Scotch heather on your hills here.'

'So these are something to do with just ordinary heather?' I ask, scarcely believing that this can be so, that there is not some more complex explanation.

'Sure,' he says. 'All one family. There's about twelve hundred different kinds of rhododendron in the genus and some of them are azaleas. Rhododendrons and azaleas are, well, kind of *cousins* to your Scotch heather. Okay then, thanks for your help. Enjoy the garden.'

And off he goes.

So I have to do some explaining. 'That's all very well, but *why* are some of them azaleas?'

'It doesn't matter,' you say. 'It doesn't matter *what* they're called, it actually doesn't.'

Your laughter takes us a good thirty yards up the path and I glance back down to see his back as he hurries on to the big house. I wonder if he'll tell Sarah about us when he meets her and what our meeting meant to him. I try to imagine myself as him as I did earlier with you, to feel his old footsteps and his precarious heartbeat, his desire to find his wife before too much more time has moved by and been wasted. I get a quick sense of this and then he turns a corner and is out of sight. I catch you up and walk with you, keeping close.

And that's really all there is to tell, except one last thing.

We come to a bench at a viewpoint looking away into the heart of Scotland, pines behind us, and down a slope and just below us is a path. We can hear, but can't see, a group of visitors being shown around by one of the garden rangers, and she's telling them all about this big *Rhododendron Protistum* and how it comes from China and how it's the largest known of all the rhododendron species and how it can grow to ninety feet tall in its native habitat. In the far distance I can see hills that I can't put a name to, blueish in the haze of the sunny day, their slopes covered with that heather, and right beside me on the bench you sit and I can lean against you and feel our upper arms press together, I can be that point of pressure. The guided group below us walks on so that we can no longer even hear them and we are alone in the garden, it seems, some distance away from the old American man and Sarah (we haven't even *seen* her) circling round each other, away from the birds picking through the yellow seaweed, away from the smooth water with the seals under the surface, and all the labels wanting to be read on the shrubs and bushes and trees, whatever they're called.

In the garden, between us and the hills, in the foreground, is a magnolia tree, its big thick pinky white petals ready to give up and let go. Around the foot of the tree the petals are piling and, as I watch, another breaks free and tumbles to the ground, touching branches and twigs, then settles quietly on top of the others. When you say we should be getting back to the car I say I want to wait on a little while here.

You see, I want to wait for one more petal to fall and I'd like to know which one it will be and where it will come to rest. I want to understand what it would be like to be that petal as the connection between me and the tree just breaks and I spin down, one moment conjoined and the next moment not, and I want to feel the air resisting me as I drop, ready to bring me to rest wherever I happen to land, and at the same time, though, I want to be here on the bench with you, watching me fall.

I believe I've never been so full of hope.

Kasia Boddy
A Story Out Of Sorts

'I began to drink heavily, think heavily, and make many heavy notes . . .'
– Hunter S. Thompson, *Fear and Loathing in Las Vegas*

'Do you think it's personal, petit bourgeois and self-indulgent?'
– Boris Pasternak, *Dr Zhivago*

'How shall I begin the story?' he asked, toes wiggling in his sandals.

To face him she swiveled on her stool. 'Say "This is a story with a happy ending."' She smiled irresistibly.

He typed aloud. '"This is a story with a happy ending," she said, "but he knew it could never be so."' He smiled irresistibly.

She swiveled again and wondered which line they would use.

They stopped resisting.

'We're a short story, ' she told him. 'A brief encounter. We come from real places to bump in this unreal one. The clocks stand still. Just one of those things.'

'And of course eventually, inevitably, we return to reality.'

'But of course,' he agreed.

'But we'll be changed, touched. Enlightened.'

'Or maybe not.' He smiled. Irresistible.

She didn't want to agree, but she smiled too.

How are they together? Apart from all the smiling?

She's too shy to say.

He's not available for comment.

Don't go breaking my heart.
I couldn't if I tried.
Dream on.

When they met she was in a blue dress, he was in red shorts. Both had bare legs. She liked his legs, as well as everything else.

He's been around the block a few times – just like his dog.

They drive everywhere, singing with the radio. They sing, 'Get out of my dreams and into my car.'

Only time will tell if they will stand the test of time.
Deep, huh?

OK. You want a story? Bored of these clever-clever comments and clichés? Well, there *is* no story. *There is no story*. They just meet, and then – in a few pages – it stops. What do you want? A list of dishes they ate together? Breakfasts, lunches, dinners. Chinese, Japanese, Thai, Italian, French. Pancakes, eggs, bagels, pizza, cups of tea, glasses of water and wine.

They argue, they sing, they sleep very close together. That's all. They aren't going to last; that's pretty clear.

But this is cold, isn't it? Where are the passions? This is supposed to be some kind of love story, for God's sake.
OK, OK. For example, she rants, she raves –
No, I can't do it.

A little distance goes a long way.

She's desperate on the phone. He can't wait to hang up.

Then the texture of others invades – thank God.

The morning after taking a morning-after pill she called a man intending to tell him that she had thrown up all night, and that it was 'his damn fault.' He complained about his indigestion.

He studied a woman in a café as she gobbled her salad, forcing leaves into her mouth, rapidly but distractedly. Her tense concentration was devoted to the book whose leaves fly as fast as the lettuce. It's title? *YOU MUST RELAX!*

She saw a man approaching with a snake. She didn't know what kind, but guessed that this might be a strangling variety. She crossed the street, walking as fast as she could without running. Later she wondered if she'd hurt his feelings.

She lay in bed with a man she didn't want to touch. But she needed a place to stay, and he seemed a gentle man. He slept better than she did, until at six-thirty she heard him get out of bed and then noises of the shower and an electric shaver. He came back to bed smelling of soap and toothpaste. She was very touched, but lay perfectly still.

She took off her earrings, so as not to scratch him as another had. He was very touched.

She stood on the doorstep in her slip, testing the temperature. A woman passed by on the step, on her way to him. Another woman called and scolded him for not calling her. Another didn't return his calls.

I hear you crying and I want to kill your friends.

But then how are they together?

They sing, they sleep very close together. They disagree about almost everything.

They tell stories of their pasts with the same compulsion as they make love. The stories don't usually make either of them very happy.

They stop telling stories.

I feel I feel I feel.

A dog looks at you, and wants to talk, and all he can do is bark. So, is this the end of the story? And is it happy or unhappy?

What could happen to make it unhappy?

They part and tell stories to their new loves about this love, which pleases no one, and it goes on – unhappily.

What could happen to make it happy?

They continue to be together, exchanging memories instead of stories, and it goes on – happily.

What could happen to make it an ending?

They spontaneously combust, and no one can be bothered to tell their story. Ha ha.

Acknowledgements to Hunter S. Thompson, Boris Pasternak, Aztec Camera, Cole Porter, Elton John and Kiki Dee, Kathy Acker, Van Halen, La Strada.

Frances Gapper
PINK AND BLUE

The first time you visited my house, I remember how pretty you looked sitting on my sofa – your blue skin against my pink cushions. You were my first blue affair, I was your first pink person, although you'd once had a green experience. I asked you, what was green like? Fey, you said, and vain. And jealous. I wasn't any of those things, I was pink. I felt glad to be pink, excited by blue.

Twiddling open my pink Venetian blinds, I introduced you to my garden – rhododendrons Pink Pearl and Sugar Pink, roses, clematis, lilies, hibiscus, pinks. Of course, not all were in flower. You politely didn't mention the green. We conspired not to admit green's existence. But you asked me, why no fuchsia (why no future?). Because, I explained, fuchsias are rarely pure pink. More often part-red or semi-purple.

You only had a window-box, in which you grew morning glories . . .

I ushered you into my pink boudoir: the essence of pinkness with its valanced-bed and dressing-table, its frilly pillows. You gasped – in admiration, I thought at first. Then, unforgivably, you laughed. Oh, very Barbara Cartland, you said.

I am in fact a distant cousin of that lady. Until you spoke, I'd been proud of the connection, the extra pink credentials it gave me. Now I shrank from your cold blue laughter. As my pinkness faded to the merest tinge, you looked a bit concerned. I mean, you said hastily, this room doesn't seem to entertain the possibility of being blue, of blueness.

Looking at you then, I saw as if for the first time how blue you were, how blue. Me pink, you blue. How strange you were to me, how utterly different from myself. Afraid and longing, I asked, what does blue mean.

We stared at each other. In your blue eyes, I saw oceans and eternities. In my pink ones, you saw I don't know what.

It means, you said. But then our lips touched – yours chilly, mine lipsticked – and from then on we spoke love, not philosophy.

I found making love to blue quite frightening. Parts of me disappeared into you and I wasn't sure if I'd ever get them back. Blue had hidden wet bits, pockets of slippery-slidiness, jelly or spawn. Like *Blue Planet*, which pink people weren't supposed to watch, but I had, and was dismayed by it. The lobster scenes were most unnerving, though filmed in a Welsh aquarium. I prefer my lobster cooked and served up to table.

The bed looked as though we'd squashed grapes in our rolling around, but I was fresh enough in love to find that delightful. The bedroom smelled richly purple, I myself like that unpleasant whiff of stale wine you get from bottle banks.

Pink was surprisingly warm and furry, you said. Like making love to a novelty hot-water-bottle. Although this didn't sound very romantic, I continued to snuggle against you, thinking sweet pink thoughts. How well pink and blue go together, the contrast highlighting our uniqueness, et cetera.

That night I dreamed in more than one colour.

You departed with airy grace. Pink nets twitched – pink shock! – as you walked down the street.

Blue, my family cried, we don't like blue. People like us don't associate with blue, or marry into it. There's nothing *wrong* with blue, they added, doubtfully. It's just not fashionable.

Lavender, lilac, violet, aubergine, buddleia and plum. My children, I thought.

But looking up at the sky, I heard my family whisper – blue is such a common colour. It's just everywhere!

One day, quite unthinkingly, I put some of your washing in with mine. The danger of colours bleeding, I didn't understand. Always wash colours separately, I'd never been advised. Oh my poor clothes, all streaky and blotched! Poor compromised me!

'I'm altered, too,' you said. 'Regrettably.'

'But you've absorbed me – see, I don't show . . .'

'You are so self-obsessed!'

This was so not true. I worried about many things that weren't myself exactly. Coral reefs destroyed by pesticides running off the land. Factory-farmed salmon.

I loved to watch sunsets. 'They kill me!' you cried. 'Pink pollutes the air.'

You refused to eat pink, I found the taste of blue repellent. We stopped having sex.

You called me fey and vain. You were jealous.

So we faded out of each others' lives. I took a pink china heart you'd given me and threw it against the wall. It shattered. It wasn't pink all through, of course, but white under a glaze. I felt doubt in my own heart – was I pink all through and forever? Or did I, like white, contain the possibility of being any colour?

Part 2

Black for train, bus and street, white my office uniform. On colour Fridays, held every two months for charity, I wore gray. They didn't know I'd been pink, once. I never blushed.

Part 3

Ill. Doctor's certificate. Lay in bed. Long time.

Part 4

A bee collecting pollen in my garden. Hanging upside down from or creeping inside a flower's narrow bell, it whined instead of buzzed. Ants performed huge tasks, shifting bits of twig and carrying seeds or crumbs or fellow ants, dead ones. The smells of rain, leaves, wet earth. Convalescence. Would I do or be anything ever again.

Part 5

A new outdoors love returned me to colour. Pale green lichen blew in tufts on thorn twigs or scaled mossy trunks. I felt as though you, green, had always been my leafy partner, the stalk upon which I flower. Yet so different!

We had an ex-lover in common. Blue, you said, was fey and vain. And jealous. Your emerald face inspired me to wonder. You showed me the pinkness of trees under their bark. Pink exists in nature, you said, it need not be anxiously cultivated. Pink balsam and spindleberries and the occasional pink leaf – oh look! you cried. Look!

Louise Tondeur

Red Roof

My hats are made from wool. Some are brown and orange, but most of them are green or grey. Once, years ago, when I was sixteen and hadn't been on the markets long, I sold hats at an outside market stall in November and it was very cold. The woman at the stall next to mine told me she was a farmer. Her smile was so big it took up half of her face. She already had a hat and it nearly covered her eyes. She looked cold and thin, but she smiled at everyone until her top gum showed. She had a thick coat on and she talked to every customer. The woman with the jumper with small strips and big glasses. The grey man with the hat and green coat. The small child with mittens and something yellow and sticky round its mouth. I only sold hats. The woman with the big smile sold everything. Slabs of cake, pots of feta, honey, plum pickle. The turnips were purple and the size of children's heads and when I curved my hand around one of them it was rough and solid. There was thick green spinach and rough carrots and parsnips curling into shapes, like they had just come out of the ground. I didn't have a tablecloth, but hers was yellow with printed roses.

She had a black dog with one ear and a grey nose which limped around her table on three good legs. The smell of the sea was in the air and I could smell it on her too. It was like her scent. She wore it along with her smile. Maybe it hung around her like a cloud. We were next to each other all day and she soon worked out that I was young and I minded her stall while she went for tea and sugar for both of us, then she told me about some of the places I had never heard of. She told me about Red Roof and said she was going to go one day again and I could come too, so it was because of the woman who smiled with her teeth and her gums that I went to Red Roof for the first time.

'Red Roof is an indoor market,' she told me, sipping her tea. I couldn't see her eyes properly, because of the way they were hidden by her hat.

'Upstairs,' she said, 'there is a room called the Top Room and if you pay you can have a space to sleep for the night and a pillow, though you need your own sleeping bag, and you get warm bread and coffee when you wake up, or honey and water. Usually the Top Room is for people who have come a long way to the market, who don't want to travel there and back again. People who want to stay to sell their things all weekend.'

The first time I went to Red Roof, it was with the smiling woman and her dog. We closed the big black door behind us and stood for a while, looking. From the doorway, I could see how big the market was. It was so big and there were so many people that I could hardly see where it ended, though I made out some stairs on the far side. We went in and my companion with the big smile, who was still wearing her hat, began to set up her stall. I didn't have my own table. A woman with a red jumper, who was in charge, told me to follow her and we pushed our way through the crowd. She showed me to a spare table in a corner, a long way from the only person in the room I knew, who waved at me and went on arranging her cabbages. On the way I saw snatches of the other market stalls, between the people, some with food, others with glass jars or clothes. The hall was big and dark and people moved around drinking cups of hot wine and spices and eating chocolate bread or gingerbread cake. I saw a girl with messed up blonde hair and fish blue eyes a few steps away from me as we went through the hall. She turned to look, but the woman in the red jumper was moving quickly and soon we were gone into the crowd of people.

I laid out my hats. On the stall next to mine, there were orange butter squash and slabs of cheese – some of it was green with herbs – and bags of garlic and white pots of olives and under the table there were big sacks of potatoes.

After a while, I left my stall in the hands of the man who owned the cheese and vegetables and went to look round. It was a witch's cauldron place, full of smells and spells and people. Light was flickering, mainly from the fire and candles, and there was a thick purple curtain hanging over a door at the back behind the stairs. The floor was made of grey stone and there was a log fire in the middle of the wall next to my table, with big arm chairs around it. While I had set up my stall, two children had bounced up and down on the chairs and stood on their heads. They were small, both girls, about two and a half feet tall, one with brown hair to her shoulders and the other with dark brown afro twisted into tight curls. And I saw one woman dancing to herself in the corner. Soft music played behind her, which I heard when I went nearer. It had a fast beat, but most people didn't hear it, so she looked like a goddess twisting to herself, with six arms and seven eyes – an eye in each hand and one on her forehead. She had black hair.

There was a counter in the corner by the door where we had come in where two women with tight white aprons and ginger hair – maybe they were sisters, I thought – served people. I went over to look. There was fruit and spice in mugs, mango and cinnamon, ginger and carrot, apple, ginger and honey, frothed up together in a mixer behind the counter.

One of the sisters smiled over at the man behind a table near by. He was selling instruments. He wore a red hat because away from the fire it was cold, and the flaps at the side came down over his ears. There were big pipes and drums with skins stretched over them. Lots of people stood around his table, so I couldn't see very well. He juggled with red and yellow juggling balls and people tried out the drums and the stringed instrument he had put at the front of the table. I wandered back to my stall and looked over to the other side of the room to where my companion with the big smile had forgotten me. She was selling a round turnip to an old man with a stick. The dog with one ear was sitting with its head on its paws in front of the table. Then when I looked back there was the girl with blue eyes I had seen before. She was playing with my hats. She had hair like sand or hair like you get when you stand on the beach with your face in the wind for so long that the salt gets mixed in with your hair and messes it up. She had blue eyes like blue fish or like the flames at the heart of the fire if you watch it and watch it until there's nothing else in your head apart from the fire and your face is hot from watching, then you might see a little blue flame under one of the burning logs and feel like Shedrach in the fire. She had eyes that were that kind of blue. She was wearing a green jumper with a white star on the front and dark blue jeans. She didn't buy a hat. I noticed when I was close to her for a second time that she was about the same age as me. She saw me looking at her and moved on to another stall. When I had finished serving a customer, she was picking up silver earrings from a different table and holding them up so she could see them and twisting them round so they caught the light. She didn't buy any earrings either. I watched her push her way through the crowd and towards the stairs. She went up quickly. I didn't see her come back down again and I thought she must have stayed in the Top Room that the smiling woman had told me about.

Even though it was still daylight outside it felt like evening inside. Once you were inside you couldn't tell whether it was day or night. Once you were inside you couldn't see the stone walls or the patterns on the outsides of the windows. Now I have been back to Red Roof a hundred times I know that there are shutters on the inside so you can't see out, but my first time when I was sixteen, I just knew it felt dark and smoky. Also, I know now that you can only see the red roof from outside, and that outside the walls are painted green and big iron letters hang on one wall. They spell out the name of the hall – Red Roof. Now I've been back again and again, I know that the hall is called Red Roof because the roof is made of red stone and it's flat so that if you climb up the stairs away from the hall where the people are and into the Top Room and if you stand on a chair and push yourself up and out of the skylight, the one next to where the chimney stack goes, if you climb up and out of the window you can stand and watch the street below if you want to. If you want to you can see the people in thick coats hurrying up the street with their hats pulled over their eyes and ears against the cold and their turnips and potatoes and slabs of cake. You can turn your face up towards the grey sky and watch the white screwed up balls of hail start to fall and crunch up your eyes and nose as they fall on your face. Balls of hail that sting like electric shocks and make you feel like you are alive and not dead. Little orgasm things falling on your face so cold you think your face might turn blue or grey like the sky and you think you might turn into part of the cloud and step off the roof and swoop over the other roof tops which aren't red but are grey like the cloud. Standing on top of the red roof you can see a blue grey line where the sea is but you can't see the orange buoys bobbing on the grey waves or the adolescent white and brown seagulls spreading their wings and hooking their beaks. Down by the sea front the sleeping masks of the yachts sing like bells in the wind. If you were there, in the winter like it is now, down by the harbour, the wind would be cold on your cheeks and the wind would blow the hail towards you from the sea and you wouldn't be able to look anymore. Or if you walked up the hill a little way from Red Roof, you would get to the top of the hill and then you could see the grey sea spread out like a picnic blanket underneath you. You could watch the night creep in around the rocks and sit still over the water from the top of that hill. You could think about the turnips with purple children's faces and think about the ice in your hair.

When you go back inside Red Roof, you'll see that some people are leaving. Some people have sat down in the chairs by the fire and have lit tightly rolled cigarettes or brown pipes that smell sweetly of herbs, and are drinking camomile and honey out of big mugs. Now people are leaving, if you listen carefully, above the fire crackling, you can hear the yachts singing in the distance, and hear the brown and white seagulls crying to themselves in the cold. The dog with one ear lies down by the fire and before he closes his eyes you can see they are milky-white and that he's old and tired. He sleeps and you can see he is dreaming when his tail moves. The fire spits and you can smell lavender from a large green pot on the hearth.

My first time, when I was sixteen, I didn't know about the harbour or the skylight or the singing yachts. When the day and most of my hats had gone, and when the hall was beginning to empty of people, I saw that the woman with the big smile who had brought me was packing up her table and her turnips. I could smell the fire and cinnamon and lavender that was left over as the people went. I looked over to the stairs. I remember thinking that the girl with the messed up hair and fish-blue eyes hadn't come back down from the Top Room. I remember a feeling like I wanted to be in the same room as her. The emptying hall felt uncomfortable without her there. I knew that the Top Room was serious because the woman with the big smile had been there before to play. And I remember wondering what they were playing that day. I wondered what her name was and whether I could get to talk to her if I played too and I hoped that I knew the game they were playing.

So when there were no more customers, I wrapped my remaining hats in the blanket I had brought to sleep on. Then I got hot apple and cinnamon from the counter and went up the stairs to the Top Room, where there was pink carpet on the floor and where a group of people had gathered around a table and weren't smiling. The girl with the sandy hair was there but she didn't look up. They were all concentrating. Only the woman in the red jumper who had shown me my table looked up when I came up the stairs. She had brown hair in a ponytail and lines around her mouth and her eyes which made her look dangerous like she knew things, but safe and warm at the same time. I sat down at a table near by with my drink steaming and stashed my hats and blanket under the chair.

I could see from the pictures on the cards that they were playing Scrummage. I felt pleased because I knew how to play because my father had taught me the cards before I could read and I wanted to join in but I didn't say anything. I watched first because I wanted to be invited. I watched the next round. I saw who had the Ghost Card from where I was sitting and I saw who had the Brown Girl but I didn't move or show it on my face. I knew better. I looked around the Top Room. Over in the corner a curtain had been hooked against the wall and I saw that behind it there were three mattresses piled one on top of the other and some thick blankets with two or three big pillows. Looking at the makeshift bed made me wonder who would get to sleep on it. It looked much more comfortable that the other rugs and mattresses and cushions thrown around the rest of the room.

Then someone on the other side of the table, the man sitting next to the woman I wanted to talk to, played the Red Jester and the spell was broken and everyone sat back in their chairs and stretched and someone lit a cigarette and someone else ran off downstairs for more tea. People laughed and yawned and gathered up the cards.

'You know it?' the woman with the red jumper asked me.

'Yes,' I said.

'Come and play.' I pulled my chair nearer.

'I'm Ann,' she said and made space for me.

'Faith,' I said. Some of the others nodded. The girl with sandy hair looked up at me but didn't nod or say anything. No-one introduced me to anyone else. They were used to knowing each other and used each other's names easily. I learnt a few straight away.

'Sit down, Patty,' the man next to me said to a big woman wearing dungarees. Patty smiled at him and sat down beside him. She had braided hair and the beads caught the light as she moved her head around.

'Simon's turn to deal,' said Ann. Simon was the man who had won the last game. It seemed as though Ann was in charge of games as well as tables. We picked up our cards. Mine weren't good. The Two of Rakes, the Yellow Feather Man and the Prince of Grass. I smoothed the cards with my thumb and wondered how many fingers had touched the pictures. I liked the colours and the way the clothes had been drawn and I imagined someone making a picture of me to put on a card and I wondered if someone did – would I be caught there on the card like a red leaf that looks like a caught butterfly in the road, or like a man trapped in a mirror.

'Your turn,' said Ann. I could feel everyone's eyes on me.

'What's her name?' I heard someone say.

'My name's Faith,' I said.

'Faith,' someone whispered.

'Scream,' I said, quietly. I had wanted to make a good impression, but now I felt very shy. I put down the Two of Rakes and picked up a card from the pile. The Knife Card. It was a red card and it might have been useful if I'd had anything higher. It wasn't a promising start. I could see the more experienced players noting behind their eyes that I didn't have good cards. I took a sip of my drink.

'Snatch,' said the man next to me and put down the Nab of Sixes. He took three more cards from the pile. Now no one was smiling. Everyone was back into the game as if they had never left it, apart from a slight feeling of difference because Ann had admitted another player.

Patty looked at her friend quickly and laid down the Man of Mirrors. It was a yellow card. The edges gleamed under the light like they were made of gold. Further round the circle someone had the Boy of Mirrors and won the hand. Everyone breathed out together. One man, who had a beard, lit a pipe. The next round began.

The girl with messy hair who's name I didn't know yet said, 'Scream.' She put down the Red Hen and picked up another card. Our discarded cards, the Two of Rakes and the Red Hen, sat side by side in the scream pile. She flashed a look at me. We were the only two screamers so far. I held onto the look she'd given me inside my head. It was good to feel her looking at me with her blue fish eyes.

Ann reached over and touched the girl's hand like she knew her well enough to touch her and for it not to be sexual or threatening but just friendly, like she'd known her for ten years and loved her easily, I thought.

'The Red Hen,' Ann said and stroked the back of her hand, 'Not so good this time, Star.' I wondered if Star was her real name or if it was a nickname. It looked from Ann's score sheet as if Star had held a lot of high risk cards early on, but had won some good hands. It looked like the game might be between Simon and her, but it was hard to tell, reading Ann's writing upside down. Then Simon smiled to himself and played the Green Jackdaw and everyone sighed and handed over their highest green cards. Reluctantly I gave up the Prince of Grass. Though the card was worthless, I liked the picture of the man in the green feathered hat with a pink sweet pea in his hand and shiny eyes. The Jackdaw was a chance to see what high cards other people had been holding onto. I knew I wouldn't win now, so I didn't take in the cards that other people passed over, although I looked at Star's card. The Green Spider. Quite good, I thought, a hard one to give up. I wondered if I could call her Star or if I had to wait until I could touch the back of her hand like Ann had done. Simon collected up his new cards and looked around the table slyly.

'Be careful, Simon,' said Patty. If someone played the Red Jester or the Ghost Card now, Simon would lose a lot of points, but when it came to Patty's turn she was a screamer too. She put the Blue Hen next to the red one.

'What are we playing for?' I whispered to Ann suddenly. I had forgotten to ask and now I wasn't going to win I felt like I could without sounding ambitious. I hoped it wasn't too serious. When I was that age, I didn't play the serious games when I came across them and I was usually careful to ask first or look at people's face's to see. This time I hadn't been so careful because I wanted to be in the same room as the girl with the messy hair. Ann motioned to the next player to put down a card.

'The bed,' said Ann simply. I looked over to the corner again, where the three mattresses were piled behind the curtain. No wonder people had looked at me uneasily when I had started to play, though, even if I had won all the remaining hands, it would be hard for me to get anywhere on the score sheet because I'd come in halfway through.

Then it was Star's turn again. She had the Red Jackdaw. She must have picked it up last time round, I thought.

'That's better,' said Ann and smiled at her. If anyone had the Red Jester they would have to hand it over. The players all waited as one by one we put down our cards. The man with the beard had it. He must have been waiting till his hand was stronger. People gasped when he had to hand it over. It was risky to play the Red Jackdaw. Now everyone knew Star could win on her next go if she wanted to. If her hand was strong enough. Anyone with the Ghost Card was likely to play it. We looked at each other. People played their strongest cards. When I put down the Knife, people pulled faces and said, 'Faith, you had it all along,' and I felt like I was part of the game. No one had the Ghost. When it was Star's turn again, Simon said, 'Go on Star' good-naturedly. She smiled and it was the first time I'd seen her smile. I noticed that she had a tiny piece of crystal fixed to one of her teeth, like an earring in her mouth. Maybe that's why she's called Star, I thought. She played the Red Jester.

'Time,' said Ann, looking at her watch.

'One more?' said Simon.

'We agreed the time,' said Ann. Everyone nodded. Ann spent a moment leaning over her score sheet, but it seemed as though people already knew the outcome. The man with the beard had gone off down the stairs for another drink and a couple of people had started chatting and shuffling their cards absentmindedly.

'Star wins on points,' said Ann.

People started to move away from the table. Some went to claim a sleeping space and some broke open big bars of chocolate. I stayed where I was at the table. Ann gathered the cards together, took the band out of her hair and wrapped it around the cards, so that her hair fell over her shoulders, then she got up and left us too. She squeezed Star's shoulder as she went past and down the stairs. The next time I saw Ann, she was sitting by the fire with a silver pipe in her hand, listening to the man with the beard tell stories. It was just Star and me at the table. She smiled again and I saw her fish eyes and the star on her tooth. I wondered how to talk to her. It would be nice, I thought, to trace the shape of her face with my finger and put my fingers in her mouth. It would be nice, I thought, to be able to see whether she was thinking about the game or the prize or me.

'I'm going to get some food,' I said, because I couldn't think of anything else, 'do you want some?' She shrugged.

'Maybe later,' she said. Not about me then, I thought, and I got up and made my way back downstairs. It was getting late and most of the people who weren't staying had gone home. I walked all the way across the hall, around the few lingerers, and the sellers packing up their things, to the counter in the corner. There was only one ginger-haired sister serving at the counter now. I ordered fried potato and cheese and sat down on a stool to wait.

'And apple, cinnamon and ginger,' I said, and put down my money. She poured me a glass and I let the steam warm up my face and the hot glass warm up my hands. I looked around the hall. The woman with the big-gummed smile had folded up her table completely and was sitting on a chair with her black dog at her feet. Although we had come together, I still didn't know what her name was. She was talking to the man who sold the instruments. He had packed all his unusual objects away and there was no sign of them. On the side of the hall near where the stairs were I could see the woman who had been dancing earlier, dancing again, with another woman this time. They looked like Gemini twins dancing together. My father showed me a picture of the signs of the zodiac once, where the Gemini twins carried water pots on their heads. I imagined the dancing women with pots on their heads, using one hand to steady them and seeing some of the water splashing over the edges and onto the floor. Over by the wall on the far side of the hall, more people sat eating corn and soup. Then I looked over to the fire and saw that Star had come back downstairs and was sitting with Ann, eating raspberries from a bowl. She must have changed her mind about food I thought and I felt jealous of the fire, because I was cold over in the corner, but I was too shy to go and sit with them without the cards to hide behind.

She must have seen me looking, because just as the ginger-haired sister put my potato and cheese down in front of me with a fork, Star got up and made her way towards me around the sacks of potatoes that still stood in the middle of the hall and the tiny sculptures of round people with big eyes and some blue bottles, which someone was packing away carefully into a case. She sat next to me. There was raspberry juice around her mouth. She ordered hot wine, but she wouldn't let me pay for it.

'You were looking at me,' she said.

'I was thinking about the fire,' I said, half telling the truth.

'Are you cold?' she said.

'A bit.'

'You've got nice hands,' she said, looking at me holding my glass. My cheeks felt hot when she said that. I looked down at my hands.

'Thanks,' I said. She smiled.

'You have to say something back now.'

'Sorry.' I wanted to say you've got beautiful eyes and your hair looks salty and I like that thing you've got in your mouth, but I didn't. Instead I said, 'You're good at Scrummage.'

'Have you got a coat?' she said.

'Yes,' I said. I had a big grey fleece, which I had hung up in the corner, near where my hat table had been.

'It's cold outside, but I want to show you.'

'Show me what?' I said. She didn't answer.

'Finish that,' she said and pointed to my dinner, 'And meet me outside.'

'Why?'

'I like you,' she said and pulled my ear slowly like she knew me already.

Outside the stars were shining through holes in the deep grey clouds and I saw the full moon once before it disappeared. We went down the hill and turned the corner and there was the sea in front of us and the yachts and the smell of sand and of crabs. We went and stood right on the edge of the harbour with our toes over the edge and looked at the boats and the rocks that curled round to make the bay. I was very cold now. Star had been warmed up by the fire before she came and still had a bit of the fire inside her. She picked up my hands and rubbed them between hers, until they were tingling.

'Now put them in your pockets,' she said and I did.

'What are you going to show me?' I said.

'Wait,' she said. Then she led me away from the harbour and over to the little stony beach that sat quietly by itself waiting for morning. The stones were covered in black seaweed because the sea had been rough earlier, though it was a little calmer now. Star looked up at the sky and said, 'More hail tonight probably.' I nodded and we went down onto the beach.

'Have you been here before?' she said.

'No,' I said. She walked along the rocks that formed the edge of the beach until she came to a shallow cave that cut into the black rock suddenly.

'Here,' she said, and she sat down inside the cave and motioned for me to sit down next to her. Then she picked up something that was lying next to where she was sitting and handed it to me. It was a skull. Probably a sheep or a goat. The skull had been worn smooth by the sea. I felt it with my hand.

'I think it drowned,' she said, and took it from me again. 'A long time ago.'

'Is that what you wanted to show me?'

'No. Just this,' she said quietly and pointed out of the cave towards the beach and the sea which was framed by the cave mouth and was grey-black and fringed with white fists, which were pummelling the stones like they were angry. The dark clouds hung over the sea like giant parachutes.

'It's beautiful,' I said, though my words were taken away by the night as soon as I had said them. They sounded too loud and next time I spoke, I spoke quietly, like she had done.

'And I want to kiss you,' she said, so quietly I could hardly hear her at all, 'but I didn't want to do it in there with everyone watching.'

'I thought you didn't want to talk to me after we played upstairs,' I said.

'I'm just shy,' she said.

'Me too,' I said and we didn't do anything. We sat looking out at the sea bashing the stones with its fists, like the beach was a door and the sea was demanding to be let in.

I turned round and saw her eyes flashing at me like fish again. Then I kissed her with the sound of the sea getting angrier in front of us. She was as soft as sand. When we looked up again, the hail had started. We linked arms and ran back to Red Roof, with the hail stinging out necks and ears and our faces tucked as far inside our coats as they would go. When we got back, most people had gone to bed. There was no one by the fire so we sat and got warm again and then we got too hot and sat back a little bit.

'Is Star your real name?' I asked. She didn't say anything. Instead she rolled up her sleeve and showed me her left arm. There was a scar from her wrist up to her elbow in one long line. I ran my finger along it. The line was softer than the skin around it and pinker.

'I fell on a broken window when I was small,' she said, 'then it was my nickname. My parents called me Scar and when I went to school, the other kids called me it too.'

'That's nasty,' I said, and I ran my finger over the scar again. It was beautiful, I thought, but I didn't say it.

'Ann's my foster Mum,' she said, 'she's in charge of Red Roof.'
'Yes,' I said.

'She said I should get a star in my mouth and tell everyone that my name is Star not Scar. So I did.' We kissed each other again for so long that the side of my face nearest the fire got really hot. I put my hand up to feel her face and she was hot too.

'I'm tired,' she said, and stood up, 'I want to go to bed.' I felt sad because I thought for a second she was going to sleep on the three mattresses without me, but then she said, 'Come on,' and pulled me up too. We climbed up the stairs together and stepped over the sleeping bodies quietly. Ann was curled up asleep in the corner on one of the small mattresses. We got onto the bed and pulled the curtain around us. I pulled the blankets into shape. We both took our trousers off quickly because it was cold, and got underneath. We could hardly see each other now the curtain was closed. She picked up my left hand and kissed it.

'You've got nice hands,' she said.

'You told me,' I said.

'You have to say something back.'

'OK, you've got nice eyes and hair and I like your shiny tooth thing and your scar.'

'You used them all up at once,' she said. I put my hands on her waist and said that no those weren't the only things. I took my top off, then I helped her lift off hers and I kissed her again and it felt like we were the same person for a long time until I opened my eyes and heard drumming on the roof and skylight and I thought it might be the angry sea wanting to get in. She put her head on my chest and I could feel her hair on my neck and smell how salty it was. It wasn't the sea. It was the hail knocking on the roof, banging so hard, and the wind, blowing so strongly that we couldn't sleep and we both lay awake in the dark with our eyes open, listening.

Egon Schiele
POETRY

Translated by Will Stone *&* Anthony Vivis

Egon Schiele was born in 1890 in Tulln, a small town on the Danube near Vienna. In 1906 he was rejected by the Viennese School of Arts and Crafts, which strongly favoured Jugendstil, and enrolled instead at the Academy of Fine Arts. In 1907 he met Gustav Klimt, and fell under the influence of Impressionism and the Vienna Secession. Two years later, to escape the Academy's emphasis on historical painting, Schiele founded the Neukunstgruppe (New Art Group). From about 1910 to 1915 he also wrote poems. After his first solo exhibition in 1911 Schiele began developing the Expressionist style – vibrant colours, angular structures, often melancholy moods – which characterizes his paintings, graphic work and poems. Living openly with Edith Harms (whom he married in 1915), and painting many young women and girls estranged him from the local community. Having just achieved recognition and material success, he died of Spanish flu in 1918.

These poems are not Rilke, Celan or Trakl – though at times the dark imagery and percussive metre recall the last mentioned. Nevertheless, Schiele's poems are striking examples of early twentieth-century Expressionist poetry. This selection of English translations will, we hope, prove Schiele's poetic gifts and encourage readers to return to the original German, also printed here.

Some poems first appeared in the pacifist pamphlet, *Die Aktion* (*Action*), published in Berlin during the First World War by Franz Pfemfert. Schiele's friend, Arthur Rossler, first published the poems in 1921, in the long out-of-print, *Egon Schiele, Prosa und Gedichte* (*Egon Schiele, Prose and Poems*). In April 1979, most of the poems were published in *Egon Schiele 1890-1918 – Leben, Briefe, Gedichte* (*Life, Letters, Poems*), edited by C.M. Nebehay.

We soon see that Schiele's poems were written by a painter, several titles evoking pictures – 'Self-Portrait' ('Selbstbildnis'), 'The Portrait of a Pale Silent Girl' ('Das Porträt des Stillbleichen Mädchens'), and 'White Swan' ('Weisser Schwan').

A poem that skilfully mixes a characteristically Expressionist palette of yellow, blue and red in unfamiliar ways is 'Abendland', which we have translated as 'The West'. The title in German evokes not only the West as such but the whole 'Occident', or the 'Hesperides', distantly suggesting the work of poet, dramatist and translator, Friedrich Hölderlin.

A similarly sedate stillness of the observed moment informs another painterly poem, called simply 'Lady in the Park' ('Dame im Park'). This also evokes Expressionist brightness of colour, reinforced by the choice of familiar imagery observed in a highly individual way.

Anthony Vivis, Norwich, 2002

Self Portrait 1

I am everything at once, but never will I do everything at once.

Selbstbildnis

Ich bin alles zugleich, aber niemals werd' ich alles zu gleicher Zeit tun.

Self Portrait 2

An interminable dreaming of life's sweetest excess –
restless – with anxious inward pain, in the soul. – blazes,
burns, alert after battle, – heart spasm. Weigh it all up –
and madly active with activated lust, – powerless is the
torment of thought, meaningless to extend thought. –
Speak the language of the creator and give. – Daemons!
Break their power! –
Your language. – Your signs. – Your might.

Selbstbildnis 2

Ein ewiges Träumen voll süßesten Lebensüberschuß –
rastlos, – mit bangen Schmerzen innen, in der Seele. –
Lodert, brennt, wachst nach Kampf, – Herzenskrampf.
Wägen – und wannwitzig rege mit aufgeregter Lust. –
Machtlos ist die Qual des Denkens, sinnlos, um Gedanken zu reichen. –
Spreche die Sprache des Schöpfers und gebe. – Dämone!
Brecht die Gewalt! –
Eure Sprache, – Eure Zeichen, Eure Macht.

Anarchist Sun

Taste, red one! Smell swaying white winds,
look hard at the universe: Sun, gold glittering
stars, look until you recover and are forced to
close your eyes. Mind worlds sparkle about you
in your sockets. Let your passionate fingers tremble,
grope for the element you must thirstily seek out,
staggering, that sits leaping, lies lurking, dreams while
resting, grows while dreaming. Fever consuming
thirst and hunger, and reluctance, blood seeps through.
Look upon me, father, upon me, you are there,
envelop me, give me: Nearness, distance, run
here and there in fury, world. – Now stretch your
noble bones. Offer me a tender ear, lovely
pale blue watery eyes. – That, father, was there.
Here I stand before you.

Anarchist Sonne

Koste Roter! rieche wiegende weiße Winde, schaue an am
All: Sonne, gelbglitzernde Sterne schaue, bis dir wohl ist
und du mußt schließen die Augen. Hirnwelten funkeln dir
um in deinen Höhlen. Laß zittern dir die innigen Finger,
taste am Elemente, der du durstig taumelnd dir suchen
mußt, springend sitzt, laufend liegst, liegend träumst,
träumend wachst. Fieber fressen Hunger und Durst und
Unlust, Blut fugt sich durch.

Wheatfield

Days radiant light reaches the wrinkled earth.
Sun breathes in and out, warming the rich soil.
Yellow areas cross steeply into the fullest green,
they grow nearer and show us here their yellow atoms,
they play through the sheer joy of life.

Ährenfeld

Leuchtendes Hellicht durchschält runzlige Erde.
Sonnen atmen auf und nieder, erwärmen reichlichen Boden.
Gelbe Flächen durchkreuzen steil ein sattiges Grün,
sie wachsen näher und zeigen uns hier die gelben Atome,
sie spielen vor Lust an dem Leben.

Damp Evening

I wanted to listen to the cool breath of evening,
the black storm trees, then the gnats, the lamenting,
the coarse footfalls of the farmers, pealing bells
in the distance, hear the regatta trees, see the competition
avenues and hear the gnats singing like wires in the
Windwinterland. But the great figure in black broke
the sound of their strings. – The raised city lay cold
in the water before me.

Nasser Abend

Ich habe lauschen gewollt des kühl atmenden Abends, der
schwarzen Wetterbäume, ich sage: der schwarzen Wetter-
bäume; dann der Mücken, der klagenden, der groben
Bauernschritte, der fernhallenden Glocken, die regatten-
bäume hören, die Wettlaufalleen sehn und Mücken singen
wie Drähte im Windwinterland. Aber der große schwarze
Mann brach ihre Saitenklänge. – Die aufgestellte Stadt war
kalt im Wasser vor mir.

Portrait of the Pale Silent Girl

A pollution of my love, – yes I loved it all.
The girl came, I found her face, her unconscious,
her worker's hands; I loved everything of her.
I had to portray her, because she has that look
and was so close. – Now she is gone.
Now I encounter her body.

Das Portrait des Stillbleichen Mädchens

Eine Pollution meiner Liebe, – ja. Alles liebte ich.
Das Mädchen kam, ich fand ihr Gesicht, ihr Unbewußtes,
ihre Arbeiterhände; alles liebte ich an ihr.
Ich mußte sie darstellen, well sie so schaut
und mir so nahe war. – Jetzt ist sie fort.
Jetzt begegne ich ihrem Körper.

Lady in the Park

And so I strode along the sun-white way –
I who was red.
I saw the blue lady in the green –
in the green garden.
She remained standing quite still –
she observed me with round dark eyes.
Her face was almost white.

Dame in Park

. . . so schritt ich den sonnenweißen Weg weiter –
ich, der ich rot war.
Ich habe die blaue Dame gesehen im Grünen –
im grünen Garten.
Sie blieb stille stehen –
sie schaute mit runden dunklen Augen auf mich.
Sie war fast weiß im Gesicht.

White Swan

Over the moss-odoured black-rimmed park lake
in rainbow spray glides the tall, quietly rounded swan.

Weisser Schwan

Über den moosriechenden, schwarzumrandteb Parksee gleitet
im regenbogenfarbenen Schaum der hohe ruhige runde Schwan.

Sensation

High vast winds turned my spine to ice
and I was forced to squint.
On a scratchy wall I saw
the entire world
with all its valleys, mountains and lakes,
with all the animals running around
shadows of trees and the patches of sun
reminded me of clouds.
I strode upon the earth
and had no sense of my limbs
I felt so light.

Empfindung

Hohe Großwinde machten kalt mein Rückgrat
und da schielte ich.
Auf einer krätzigen Mauer sah ich
die ganze Welt
mit allen Tälern und Bergen und Seen,
mit all den Tieren, die da umliefen –
Die Schatten der Bäume und die Sonnenflecken erinnerten
mich an die Wolken.
Auf der Erde schritt ich
und spürte meine Glieder nicht,
so leicht war mir.

The West

I saw swaying fields cut through with tiny spikes
by a thousand vanishing points to yellow,
mirror ponds and tender clouds.
Inclining mountains arched over and enclosed
the air in veils.
I smelt the sun.
Now the blue evening had come
sang out and only then revealed the fields.
A red glow still enshrouded a blue mountain
I was dream surrounded by the many-scented.

Abendland

Ich habe Schaukelfelder durch winzige Zacken zerschneiden gesehen
von Tausenden verlierenden Punkten auf Gelb.
Spiegelteiche und weiche Wolken.
Neigend bogen sich die Berge und hüllten
Lüfte aus Schleiern ein.
Ich roch die Sonne.
Jetzt war der blaue Abend da,
sang und zeigte mir erst die Felder.
Einen blauen Berg umfloß noch roter Schein.
Ich war von all dem Vielduftigen umträumt.

Country Road

The lofty trees all walked along the road.
In them tremulous birds chirped.
With great strides and red-eye anger
I raced down the dank highway.

Lanstrasse

Die hohen Bäume gingen alle die Sraße entlang.
In ihnen zirpten zittrige Vögel.
Mit großen Schritten und roten Bösaugen
durchlief ich die nassen Straßen.

image: gregg potter
<tupper61@hotmail.com

Stephen Chamberlain

AIRPORTS DON'T COUNT

An electronic sign scrolled out the word 'Berlin' over and over, and too many people were smoking too many cigarettes in a room that already smelled like it had been dead for a thousand years. Another reason, he decided, why he disliked airports – the people who use them.

A hastily-caught flight out of a connecting city he never knew existed to a stopover in another place he didn't want to know, followed by an unscheduled layover wherever the hell this was. He had been flying for three days straight, he never wanted to see the sky from the top down again. But he had someplace called home which he had to get to and a job interview which could mean many things – all of them good. And that meant he had to keep moving.

Max looked down at the rectangle of plastic which he had been given by a disinterested man as he left the fetid tube of the plane with the seat of his trousers sticking to his backside. The transit card looked back at him, devoid of any meaning. None of the signs about the room were in a language he understood, and anyone who was talking was murmuring just below the threshold of audibility.

Standing in an arrivals lounge that was his idea of the passive-smoking room from hell and seeking advice from a piece of plastic was not going to get him anywhere, so he pocketed the plastic and looked around him. The place was your basic airport generic: marble floors scuffed of any shine they used to have, concrete pillars, signs hanging from high ceilings which were rough and unpainted and walls which you didn't want to lean against. The sign scrolling out the word 'Berlin' seemed to have used up all the letters of the alphabet except those it now repeated endlessly.

Max watched and watched, hoping it would tell him what to do. But after too long he began to suspect that although Berlin was what it said, it didn't mean the city – rather it was just how the letters had randomly come together. A suspicion confirmed when, imperceptibly, it changed to read 'Nibnerl'.

Berlin would have been a giant step closer to home, though, and he regretted its passing. At the thought of home, he patted the back pocket of his trousers absentmindedly. The letter about his interview was still there – a comforting talisman and a focus of his efforts to get moving, keep moving and get back.

Max moved away into a narrow corridor which led into another large room exactly like the last, except no one was smoking. Another sign listed what were presumably flight details in an alphabet that may have been Cyrillic, but wanted to be European and still meant nothing to him.

And there were no windows.

Another corridor led to a dark and lifeless shopping mall bottled up behind a wall of barred shutters. The whole terminal appeared to be arranged in a doughnut shape with the mall in the centre. The lighting was septic, it scratched his eyeballs. There were no clocks so it was not possible to tell the time of day. His watch was in a time zone of its own and the hands had fallen off his body clock.

A woman passed him. Sallow and unsmiling, she had a bucket in one hand.

He found his voice, 'Could you tell me where the information desk is?'

She peered up at him and said, 'Eh?'

'The information desk,' he asked again.

She shrugged. He became monosyllabic.

'Information.'

'Eh?'

'Help?'

'Eh?'

'Authority.'

'Authority?' She sounded each syllable slowly, her pronunciation slightly to one side of correct, like the right tune with the wrong notes.

'Yes. Authorities. Where are the authorities please?' He asked.

'Oh yes, there is authority here.' And she walked off.

Max followed her for two or three impatient steps, determined to gain an answer, but then he threw up his hands, 'Fine, walk away,' but he didn't say it very loudly; the last thing he wanted was a scene in a foreign airport which could delay him even more. So much was riding on him being able to get moving again, but he'd been in this kind of situation dozens of times before. He could handle it.

He noticed a bank of seats where a couple sat silently. Neither looked up as he approached and he had to stand right in front of them to get their attention. 'I'm sorry, but do you know when the next flight out of here is? Or maybe where I can find the information desk?'

As soon as he spoke, the woman began to cry. The man simply stared at the floor, rocking back and forwards.

Feeling slightly ridiculous standing before the distressed couple, Max escaped to another bank of seats and flopped down into one. But he couldn't think straight, he was too flustered, and he was also hungry, or maybe just in need of something to take away the dry taste of desperation. Focusing on food gave him something achievable in the short term, and he was suddenly galvanised. He found a wide entrance into what looked like a food court. Smells which could have been food-like in origin were indeed leaking out and he was drawn in.

Inside was a low-roofed, box-like room with a layer of cigarette smoke rubbing against the ceiling, making halos out of each of the eight bare bulbs which hung down at different heights. All along one side was a glassed-in food counter with painfully bright yellow lights inside, presumably for keeping the food warm. He presumed this because there wasn't any food. There was just row on row of greasy racks crusted with the remains of food which had been deep-fat fried once too often.

Approaching the counter he saw a small woman in a dirty yellow tunic lurking behind. She didn't seem to notice him at first so he rapped on the hot glass with a knuckle which throbbed from the heat for some minutes afterwards. She threw a look in his direction and inclined her head slightly.

'Food?' asked Max, to which she simply swept a hand before her, indicating the counter.

Peering through gunk-stained glass, he saw a small pile of – well, he wasn't sure what exactly they were. Maybe sausage rolls if you took out the sausage and substituted a grey mash, and then replaced the pastry with a something that looked like stale marzipan.

He pointed towards them, being careful not to touch the hot glass again. The woman shuffled along and looked out at him through the clouded barrier. Even she looked surprised that someone would want to purchase these particular items. However, he insisted and she poked them into a used plastic bag and slapped the package on top of the counter.

Max hefted a roll of random currency saved from a hundred different trips to as many countries. He always kept it handy in case such a situation arose and he needed mysterious money which carried pictures of heavy-set men in military uniform.

He peeled off several different bills and waved them hopefully.

'Dollars.' She demanded. 'Dollars.'

Again, Max was prepared. He always travelled with a wad of low-denomination US dollars on him. Now he slipped one from the top and slid it over the counter. He watched the paper going translucent as the grease soaked into it.

She held her hand out.

'Okay, okay,' groaned Max. 'How much, five, ten?' He took half the bills and tossed them at her. This time her hand darted out, enfolded the stuff and palmed it out of sight.

There was plenty of choice of where to sit – only one man was in the place, hunched in one of the corners with his back to the room, a cigarette unravelling itself in his fingers.

Choosing a random table, Max dumped the bag and heaved himself into the plastic chair which was surprisingly comfortable – a welcome change from the aircraft seat he was still recovering from.

Sadly the food was no surprise, it tasted like it looked. He made it half way through the third item before pushing the lot away with a heavy heart and a greasy hand. He felt worse than when he'd started, hunger would have been a better alternative.

Enclosing his forehead in one hand he rested his eyes for a short time. But the lure of relaxation was too much and he pressed his head onto his folded arms on the table.

He awoke with a start. The food lay heavy and merciless in his stomach like nothing would ever digest it. There was a thin veil of sweat on his forehead, and he could feel the pattern of the cloth from his suit sleeve on his cheek. He was no more rested and had no clue as to how long he had lain asleep.

Looking round he could find no sign of the woman who had served him, and the place was empty of any other customers. Nervously he patted down all of his pockets and various hiding places for money, passport and tickets. Everything was still there, but something was wrong, he was sure he had lost something . . . wait, 'Just the jet-lag,' he whispered out loud in an effort to comfort himself. Just the jet-lag.

But the words sounded a lot wilder in his mind. He could have been asleep for hours, he could have missed a message, information, anything that may have helped. Sitting around wasn't going to help. He began to run, but he wasn't thinking where he was going. No one remarked on his passage, no one got angry when he bumped into them.

But the panic gave way to nausea as he ran and the taste of the food he had just eaten rose into his mouth. He crashed through a toilet door, a wave of urine-soaked hot air broke over his head and left him vomiting on sticky floor tiles.

Silence slowly descended, along with a fusty heat which brought instant pricks of sweat to all parts of his body.

In an attempt to regain composure and control he stripped off his jacket and tie with the speed of a conjurer snatching the tablecloth from under the crockery, and stuck his head under a stream of cold tap water. Slowly it turned tepid, then lukewarm and finally began to smell brackish.

Spluttering upright he brushed the water from his eyes and stepped up to the hand-drier. However, the sensor which activated it was placed in such a way that the hot air missed his hands, and when he moved them into the stream of air, it turned off abruptly. He balled his suit jacket up in a silent rage and threw it blindly into one of the closets.

Then he thought better of tossing it aside and went to fish it out. But the jacket lay on the floor with one arm hooked over the lip of the toilet bowl so it looked like the torso of a man searching for support. There was sodden tissue paper smeared all over it. Max flushed the cistern. As he walked out the arm bobbed and spasmed in the flow like it was imploring him to return.

Walking out of the toilet door, Max was surprised to see a man in a beige uniform sitting behind a tall desk at the entrance to a corridor that led to the next hallway. From under his absurdly peaked cap the official seemed to be directing people to walk the way they were already heading. No one was overlooked or ignored.

Max approached, and sure enough, he lifted an arm to indicate the passage which turned away to his right.

'Yeah, uh . . . right. I wonder if you could help me?' Max said.

The official frowned and spoke a sentence in a language Max couldn't understand.

'I'm sorry do you speak English?'

The official shook his head and said, 'Sometimes.'

Max asked him about any flights which might be leaving soon.

Again he didn't understand the reply, but he was encouraged to be having a conversation of sorts.

Max rubbed his chin, noticed the surprisingly long growth of sharp scrub poking through, and wondered how long he'd been there now. Had he slept some of the time? He really couldn't recall.

Pulling himself back to the situation in hand he asked, 'My flight. I need to find out when my flight leaves.' He made a mime of a plane flying with his hands, and then wondered what had made him do such a thing.

The official watched his actions from beneath the impenetrable peak of his hat.

'Fly. I need to fly,' persisted Max. 'I have an important job, it needs me. Or, rather, I meant to say, I need it, I need that job. I need to be flying, moving. Going up. I need to go up. I must get on.'

The official shook his head, the huge, shiny black peak swishing through the air millimetres above his hidden eyes.

'It is not possible,' he said at length.

'But how do I get out of here?' Max pleaded.

The official stared impassively at Max, the white strip-lighting casting a crazy shadow of absolute blackness over the place where his eyes should be.

'What about information? Can you tell me where airport information is?'

Impatiently the official flicked a hand down the corridor, back in the direction Max had come.

'There?' Max jerked a thumb over one shoulder, but was so confused that he nearly punched himself in the windpipe with his forearm. 'Show me,' he demanded.

The official rose stiffly and held out a manicured hand.

'Passport,' he said firmly.

Max took a step back. There was no way he was going to surrender his passport to anyone in this place. It could be the end of him, stuck here along with all the other lonely air travellers who'd become reluctant junkies of flight. He would never get out.

Walking backwards carefully, Max left the official behind. He thought he saw a smile of victory appear on the man's face, but with a final step Max was away from him and into the great marble-floored hall with its faded colours and smells of midnight despair.

He flopped into a coarse brown chair. The fusty odour of age and cigarette smoke jumped in the air all around him and slowly began to settle all over him.

His drooping eyelids told him it was late, but time was meaningless here. His body had transcended numbers, but his mind was starving for a digit that would tell him what to do.

His head touched the cloth on the back of the seat, it itched and scratched, but it was the most comfortable part of him. The last thing he saw was a huge advertizing hoarding for Marlboro cigarettes. However, half of it was missing so it just said 'boro', and Max thought, yes, he would like to burrow somewhere.

He slept.

And he awoke.

A small ineffective whining noise turned out to be a man on the other side of the hall pushing a vacuum cleaner shaped like a

Sputnik – round and silver with the hint of an antennae.

'Get me a drink,' he mumbled out loud and snatched himself upright.

The sign was finished. To the 'boro' half had been added the words 'Marl', but not, unfortunately, in the right order. An image of the requisite cowboy on a horse enjoying his habit sat below a word which read 'boroMarl'. A line beneath him on the second half of the poster was intact, it said, 'The big country'. The cowboy had a rough face and an even rougher beard. Max rubbed his own face and was startled to find he too very nearly had a beard, yet it hadn't been so the long the last time he checked. Or he thought so anyway.

'Here, take a pull of this,' said a voice.

Max spun around at the unexpected intrusion of someone he could understand. A nondescript grey man in a business suit, slightly creased but serviceable, was offering him a huge duty-free bottle of whisky. Max grabbed it and felt the cool glass take the heat out of his palm even as the liquid burned a path through his throat to his stomach and put the right kind of warmth back. He coughed a lot and took another swig.

'My saviour,' he croaked.

'Airports, huh?' The man said in an understanding way.

'Too many,' answered Max.

The stranger nodded and gazed up at the advertising hoarding, 'You know they don't count?' he said.

'What's that?'

'Airports don't count,' said the stranger, 'for travel purposes, airports are not countries,' he added.

Max shrugged.

'When you land at Moscow airport, stay five hours and catch a plane out, you haven't been to Russia. Airports don't count,' he elaborated.

'Too depressing,' sighed Max, 'all that effort, that . . . suffering,' he felt justified in the use of the word, 'can't be for nothing.'

'On the contrary. They make them like that so the time wasted in an airport isn't really time. Nothing counts in an airport – not even wasted time. Otherwise we would be all insane after a few years of travel.'

Max indicated the bottle, received it, tilted his head and swallowed slightly more than was wise. He raked the back of his hand across his lips in the customary spirit-drinker's manner and noticed that half the liquid was gone. Had it been full when he started?

The stranger continued, 'Where we are now is a kind of geographical no-man's-land. You have come and you have gone, but you have been nowhere. So you have wasted nothing.'

The whisky was in to Max well and truly now, so he smiled and nodded. Then he remembered, 'I'm finding it hard to get out of here. It's very important that I get out of this place, I have an interview which could . . . well it's in this letter, if you'll just take a look you'll see what I mean.' He fumbled the creased envelope out of his pocket, extracted the letter and waved the paper at the man.

'Take it. Go on, take it,' Max said and let go of it.

Both men watched as the letter wafted gently to the carpet between them.

'That's done it,' said Max sadly and bent to try and retrieve it. But the man reached a hand out to stop him, 'I understand. Come with me if you want.'

Max, frozen halfway between the floor and chair, looked up in total surprise. 'You mean it?' The man nodded with a smile and extended his hand. From Max's vantage point it looked like the hand of some benign god stretching down to him from the heavens. He took it.

They found their way to a departure lounge. A few chairs were scattered around a desk placed at the entrance to a tunnel which, Max assumed, led to an aircraft. A few other people were waiting.

Max became aware of an insistent buzzing noise, in his drunken state he thought it was a fly and began swatting the air around his head. 'Damn it,' he muttered, but it carried on.

The stranger eased Max into a chair.

'Not long now.'

The buzzing had turned into a high-pitched, energetic whine and Max tried to focus his eyes and find it. At length he traced the noise back to the man with the Sputnik-like vacuum cleaner – the same uniformed man who had asked for his passport earlier.

The man walked up to the departure lounge, pushing the head of the cleaner before him, sucking a narrow path of cleanliness to tread on in the same way a member of royalty might have rose petals strewn before him. He went up to the desk, unhooked a rope barrier and stood next to the tunnel leading to the aircraft.

'Let's go,' said the stranger and Max did his best not to lurch too heavily as they walked to the queue.

From beneath the shade of his cap the uniformed man took the stranger's documents, scrutinized them and waved him on. The stranger trotted away down the passage. Max handed over his documents, but the man stiffened and would not accept them.

'You have been drinking, I think,' he said.

Max blinked at him, and then laughed a little.

'It is not a laughing matter, I think. We do not allow persons who have consumed too much alcohol on board flights.' He folded his arms and tilted his head back slightly. The shadow over his eyes did not move.

Max looked down the tunnel at the stranger with his bottle of whisky and tried to attract his attention.

'But . . . my friend, he can tell you, I haven't . . .'

'Friend? I think you have no friend here,' said the man.

'But, I tell you, he's just gone on board, if you go and ask him, he can tell you.'

'His name.'

Max had no idea what the stranger's name was. 'But he's down there.' He made a step in the direction of the tunnel but the uniformed man put a hand on his shoulder. Max turned, 'I have an appointment to get to. A job interview, look, I have a letter, you'll see everything is in order.' He fished desperately in his back pocket for the letter, but he couldn't find it, yet he was sure he'd had it with him recently.

'I think you will stay.'

'No!'

Max broke away and stumbled down the corridor. They weren't going to stop him – it was too important for him to get home, he had wasted enough time.

Behind him there were shouts and footsteps. He rounded a corner and skidded to a stop as he saw there was a ten-foot gap between the aircraft door and the extendible access tube. The plane was leaving. He teetered on the edge and watched as he and the tube moved further from the aircraft. The face of a steward stared at him from behind an oval window. He could see rows of empty seats.

'No! I need to be on that plane,' Max yelled.

He turned, trying to find the controls to extend the tunnel again, the uniformed man was standing behind him brandishing the tube of the vacuum cleaner.

'Dog!' The man snorted, taking a swipe at Max's head, but he ducked under it and fell over.

Rolling back, Max felt one leg dangle in mid-air and realised he was about to fall out of the tunnel. Looking round he just had time to see the asphalt rushing to meet him. The impact was cruel and he lay with his eyes wide and lungs winded.

Above him the man peered down, spat on him and disappeared. The tunnel moved back and Max thought he heard the word 'dog' being uttered from a long way off.

He was left alone staring at the sky where, lifting higher and higher into the vastness until it was a tiny cross nailed to the underside of the clouds, was an aircraft that might have been his.

Then it dissolved into the blankness.

image: east anglian film archive
<eafa@uea.ac.uk>

Graham Mort
POETRY

My Father's First Day at Work

Half asleep in the grey smudge of September
rain a carthorse sneezes towards fleeting
dazzles of the sun.

Its hooves click on a cobbled yard, its hide
flinches from my hand and rain trails its silver
filaments from tilted hooves.

The horse dreams me from its sweat of sleep.
Or I dream the horse, the day itself.
That smell of soap and leather,

a fly entering its nostril, this mane tangling
my fingers, the way its neck is coarse, hot,
and kissable with rain.

If I try to look away from these lost days
a boy distracts me, enters the yard
to set down pails of milk

and smiles towards me through a looming war
and does not recognize me and hardly tastes
the bit of work between his teeth.

Presence

Snow in all the windows. Two hundred miles
of steel. Delays. A burning head where
he's hammered too much gin.

Wheels thrum, water gleams in ditches,
winter's dregs spilling in a mind full of other
winters, other journeys, days.

A man at a canal yells to his Alsatian bitch;
the backs of brick-built houses pass and people
somehow keep on living there.

Maybe if he watches he'll see a shutter pulled,
a killer's hands shadowed at the throat
of some impossibly lovely girl.

But the man opposite needs to talk, unhooks his
Walkman, bringing a tinnitus of slide guitar
played the way only Texans can:

so slow, and so mean. The train enters a white-
out where fields should be green and English,
but snow's fever is forgetting them.

The ring-pull hisses. He pours tonic water's
quinine dose. Mosquitoes zing in a reed hut;
a Portuguese prospector dies in his delirium

of wealth. The river takes away rubber and
gold dust; the Indian is tattooed blue, the
dugout's prow turns water's bronze.

Rails syncopate. The man opposite describes
a Japanese border back home where he's planted
celandines, a rare foxglove. Back home.

The tonic water can rolls to the table's edge;
they gulp heated air, then brakes are
laid on hard, their balm of stasis.

A train-full of people shudders and slows,
scattering their thoughts beyond a place's
stark, enamelled name.

He's listening to the names of flowers,
imagining a garden, a woman he could
love walking by the pond's fringe of

irises, the centre of each eye wide with
longing. He notes the man's lank hair,
endures his low, legato voice.

There is something between them now,
something that only speech has built. He sips
gin's juniper sting, wonders what kind

of thing that is, how much more real than
the stairs to his room, the bed where a novel
still lies open for his mind to write in;

where sheets are scented with a presence that is
not flowers or woman, that fits him close as
sweat or a suit of darkest clothes.

Later

I have you dressed in blue, Victoria plum,
a dark old bruise, a dress of fine-spun wool,
its patina of age.

I remember this, your hand held up,
plucking out some word, some jagged
stone you couldn't spit.

Your eyes are almost lost, shadowed in
a room which smells of orange peel,
almonds, the must of bundled suits
that you've brought home again.

Memory floods, spins to a small pool
in which you move towards me dressed
in indigo, hands veined around that fruit,
that hidden gist, perhaps the clenched
word you need to place in mine.

It's not that I remember all you couldn't
say or let go of, that's not it.

But when I touched your arm, mouthing
that useless thing – which fates are best
in the end – your heart's struck fish leapt
to knock away my hand.

Sidura Ludwig
THE MEETING

This morning, for the first time, Carol realizes she has her mother's hands. She reaches for the toothpaste and, down the hall, she hears her daughter Sarah doing the same, turning on the water, moving the toothbrush across her teeth as if trying to untangle knots. The bristles scrub over nine-year-old enamel.

I will have to remind her not to brush so hard, Carol thinks as she unscrews the top of her own paste. And that's when she sees it. Her mother's hand unscrewing the top for her. As if she comes up behind her, takes the toothpaste right out of her hands and says, 'Here, let me.' And then her mother's hands spread the paste onto her toothbrush, mint gel resting gently on thin white pillars. Carol had never realized how long her own fingers are, or how they curve slightly when she tries to keep them straight. The soft sunlight, sneaking through her bathroom window, illuminates some soft, brown spots on the back of her hands. She hasn't been looking after her nails. Broken and lopsided, they look brittle and naked, cut so close to her skin. These are her mother's aging fingers and as she brushes her teeth, she wonders how they ever found themselves onto her hands. And why this morning?

At breakfast, Sarah swings her legs under her chair. She kicks the kitchen table leg with each swing while eating her cereal.

'Mum, you have to have some breakfast too.' Sarah's shoulders hunch over her bowl.

'Sit up straight, honey.'

'Mum, aren't you going to have some toast?'

'A little later.'

Carol watches Sarah's hands, raising the spoon to her lips,

holding it steady as she sucks the cereal into her mouth. Her fingers are still pudgy with bits of baby fat around her knuckles. But she has wide nail beds, healthy looking, naturally pink.

'Mum, I'm going to win the spelling bee today.'

Chocolate milk rests on top of Sarah's upper lip. Carol reaches over to wipe it off with a tissue.

'I'm sure you'll do very well. You're a good speller.'

'Yesterday I spelled 'disappointing.' Justin got it wrong. He thought there were two s's.'

'Can I put your hair back in a pony tail today?' Sarah's hair is a mess of auburn waves and curls. Her bangs are too long and Carol hates the way they fall into her eyes, like curtains.

'No, I like it like this.'

'But Sarah, it's all over your face.'

'Mum, I like it like this.'

Was I ever that stubborn? Carol thinks, clearing Sarah's bowl from the table. Outside a car honks, and Sarah rushes to put on her snowsuit. She calls goodbye from the front door and blows her mother a kiss. Carol waves, her long fingers stretched out high in front of her.

She is usually rushed in the morning, getting Sarah off to school and then herself to the office before her first client. Nothing in Winnipeg is too far, but in the winter you have to budget an extra ten minutes to warm up the car. She is not one to be late for anything – she hates to keep people waiting – but this morning she keeps glancing at the clock, telling herself another five minutes won't hurt. She cleans Sarah's dish, then all the left-over dishes from last night's supper. She scrubs away ketchup stains and dried, crusted cheese. When all of the dishes are done, she starts to dry them too. Carol hates doing dishes. Behind her the clock reads twenty to nine. She leaves the rest to dry in the dish rack and as she walks away, her heart begins to flutter.

Last night she called her mother after supper.

'So I'll pick you up tomorrow at nine, OK Mum?'

'At nine? Oh. I don't know. I don't know if I can get up on time.'

'Kristina will make sure that you're up, Mum.'

'It's awfully cold out. And icy. I'm not sure I should be outside.

My legs have been shaky.'

Carol rubbed her hand across her forehead as she held the phone between her shoulder and her ear.

'You'll be in your wheelchair, Mum. I won't let you fall.'

She heard her mother laugh, a quick, nervous puff of air.

'Where are you taking me?'

Carol closed her eyes.

'I'm taking you to the doctor's, Mum. Remember? I made you an appointment. We have a meeting with the doctor.'

'Oh, you do?' Then she sighed. 'You know me. I get so muddled.'

When Carol drives up to the apartment, Kristina has her mother bundled in her winter coat, sitting snug in the wheelchair inside the building lobby. Carol lives only five minutes from her mother, and the car windows are still defrosting when she stops in front of the building.

Kristina wheels her out. Her hands are folded on her lap. Her shoulders are hunched forward and her head is bent to one side. She gets so pale in the winter, except for her cheeks, which have been kissed permanently pink by February winds, and the stale, hot air of her apartment.

'Mrs Levy had some difficulty getting out of bed this morning, didn't you Mrs Levy.'

This is a statement, not a question, and Carol's mother answers, 'Yes,' without really listening.

'It's very cold out, today,' she says, as Kristina lifts her from the wheelchair and sits her in the passenger seat in the front. 'There's a strong wind.' Then she laughs a little, 'I hope I don't fall over.'

Carol folds the wheelchair and fits it in the back seat. She is amazed at how quickly she folds it. As if it were a baby doll's stroller.

'I won't let you fall over, Mum,' she says.

'What's that? Who's there?'

Carol closes the back door and crouches down beside her mother.

'Mum,' she says, placing her gloved hand on top of her mother's knee, 'I said, I won't let you fall.'

'Oh, hello dear,' her mother responds, 'I didn't know you were there.'

Carol turns the heat up on high as she pulls out of the driveway. Her mother lives on Wellington Crescent, in a community of condominiums that back onto the Assiniboine River. The trees that line the street are bare, but the branches are lined with a thin layer of frost that glows, along with the confetti snow at their bases. Carol drives slowly, careful not to get caught by any black ice. Her mother doesn't speak. She looks out the window as they pass the park, the snow heavy atop picnic tables, as if the tables are hibernating. She doesn't say a word when they stop at the red light next to the synagogue. Carol looks at her mother, looking out the window but not really watching anything.

It's only when they're at the doctor's office, past the Misorcordia Clinic where Carol's mother used to work as a clerk, past Enid's café on Sherbrooke where she used to have her coffee, when she finally says, 'Where are we going again?' Carol parks the car and turns off the motor.

'It's very cold,' her mother says.

'Mum, we're going to the doctor's. You have an appointment with the doctor today, and that's where we're going. I'm going to get your wheelchair out of the back and then help you into it. You're not going to fall. OK?'

Her mother smiles and pats her hand. 'You're very good to me, dear.'

The doctor's office smells like cough syrup and the air is warm and stale. Carol doesn't like the walls, baby-bonnet yellow with gold-framed prints of bouquets and pastel ice cream cones. She doesn't like the way the magazines are scattered around in uneven piles, pages worn. You can tell they've been here a while. Carol wheels her mother to a corner by a window. The view is the parking lot, and from the seventh floor, the cars look like children's toys. Her mother doesn't look out the window.

'It's very warm in here,' she says.

'I know, Mum. Let me take off your scarf for you.'

Her mother's knitted scarf and tam were a birthday present

from Sarah. She saved her allowance for three months in a spaghetti sauce jar. Carol took her to the Bay on a Saturday afternoon and she chose bright purple.

'Because that's the colour that queens wear,' she said. It had been a long time since Carol thought of her mother as a queen.

A young nurse brings them into the examining room. She has very skinny ankles and she calls Carol's mother 'dear'.

'There you go, dear. Now you put on this gown and the doctor will be with your shortly. Alright, dear?'

The nurse's hair is long, spiral-permed, and hangs down past her breasts when she places the dressing gown on Mrs Levy's lap. She smells like strawberries.

'We'll be fine, thank you,' Carol says, holding back a 'dear' that dangles dangerously from her tongue. She waits until after the nurse and her skinny ankles leave before helping her mother into the gown.

'Now, what's all this?' Mrs Levy asks, as Carol unbuttons her top.

'You have to put on this dressing gown so that the doctor can see you,' she says.

'Oh.' Mrs Levy pauses. 'Well, I didn't realize this was a, what-do-you-call-it, you know, a formal event.'

Carol can't help but smile as she ties the gown behind her mother's hunched back. Her mother smells like Ivory soap, even right behind her ear. And her thin hair brushes against Carol's cheek as she moves away.

'Well, Mum. Mint green always was your colour.'

'What's that?'

'I said, mint green always was your colour.'

'It was?'

When Carol was a girl, her parents went to the symphony every Saturday night. Her mother had two symphony outfits. One was black, with beading at the neckline, and one was mint green – a sheath that fell just above her knee. She wore it with a string of pearls and a gold watch. And heels. Black patent heels that made her tall, almost powerful.

When her mother got dressed, Carol sat on the bed and watched. Each weekend her mother let her try on a different colour of lipstick – Autumn Leaves, Midnight New York, Fire-Engine Red. Then, while her mother put on her jewellery, Carol blew exaggerated kisses into the mirror, her lips puckered like a fat rose.

Once when her father wasn't feeling well, Carol was her mother's date for the symphony. Her mother wore the green dress and Carol her black velvet, the one she wore for High Holidays that year. She put on her Mary Janes and tap danced in the front hall while she waited for her mother to put on her coat.

'Now, don't you two let any young gentlemen take you home and steal you away from me,' her father called to them as they climbed into the cab. Carol blew him kisses as they drove away down the block.

Her mother held her hand as the cab drove up slowly to the concert hall front doors.

'You stay close to me when we're inside because it's crowded,' her mother said.

'I feel like a princess,' Carol whispered.

Her mother laughed. 'I guess that makes me a queen.'

It was January, and light snowflakes floated down from the sky like dandelion seeds. As she stepped out of the cab, Carol looked up and imagined God picking dandelions and blowing the seeds over the Earth for good luck.

'Mrs Levy, I'm Dr Gerrard.' The doctor introduces himself as he opens the office door.

Carol doesn't like him yet. He's young, maybe thirty-two, and he doesn't look her mother in the eye. He opens her chart and makes notes.

'How old are you, Mrs Levy?'

'Oh my. I guess I'm seventy-five.'

Carol pats her mother's hand. 'She was eighty last month.'

The doctor nods.

'Mrs Levy, do you know what month it is?'

'It's winter. And I hope it doesn't last long,' she answers. Carol watches her mother's hands tense as she stretches out her fingers.

'What did you have for breakfast this morning, Mrs Levy?'

For as long as Carol can remember, her mother has had an orange for breakfast. Every morning, and just an orange. Her mother wrings her hands tight and she looks at her lap.

'Toast?' she whispers, 'I think.'

Dr Gerrard takes her blood pressure. He listens to her heart and has her take deep breaths as he moves the stethoscope up and down her back. With each breath, Carol's mum stares at the door in front of her but not really looking.

When he is done, Dr Gerrard takes his glasses off and closes the chart.

'Mrs Levy, do you know why you're here?'

'For the meeting,' she answers.

'Mrs Levy, we think you are a candidate for the Sharon Home. We think it's a better place for you to live than your apartment. And I'm going to suggest to them that they put you on their waiting list.'

Carol watches her mother sit up straight in her chair. For the first time, she looks the doctor in the eye and smiles with recognition.

'You've been very kind, but no thank you. I'm not going.'

The doctor looks to Carol who covers her mouth. She is smiling, but her eyes well up with tears. She has to swallow the laugh that is desperate to escape from her throat.

'Should we talk later?' the doctor asks her. Carol nods, but in her head she says, 'No thank you.' In her head, she wheels her mother out of the office, away from the hospital, far away from the Sharon Home. In her head, her mother stands up from the wheelchair, reaches out her hand and beckons for Carol to follow. In her head, they walk out of the office together.

Carol helps her mother on with her clothes after the doctor leaves.

'You sure told him, Mum.'

'Told who?'

'The doctor. You gave him a piece of your mind.'

'Yes, well, you know. Sometimes you have to do that. And my mind, you know, it's in pieces.'

In the elevator, Carol does her mother's coat up, slowly, her fingers caressing each leather button. And then her mother reaches up and touches her cheek. Her wrinkled hand is cold and thin, but it holds her face firm.

'You're so good to me,' she says.

As the doors open, Carol wheels her mother outside. Snow falls lightly, dusting the hard pavement. They stop there for a while, Carol holding firmly on her mother's chair, her mother looking up at the sky, letting the flakes land on their shoulders, their gloved hands.

Margaret Atwood

OWL AND PUSSYCAT, SOME YEARS LATER

So here we are again, my dear,
on the same shore we set out from
years ago, when we were promising,
but minus – now – a lot of hair,
or fur or feathers, whatever.
I like the bifocals. They make you look
even more like an owl than you are.
I suppose we've both come far. But

how far are we truly, from where we started,
under the fresh-laid moon, when we plotted
to astound? When we thought
something of meaning could still be done
by singing; or won, like trophies.
I took the fences, you the treetops, where we
hooted and yowled our carnivorous
fervid hearts out, and see,
we did get prizes: there they are,
a scroll, a gold watch, and a kissoff
handshake from the stand-in
for the Muse, who couldn't come herself,
but sent regrets. Now we can say

judicious things about each other
on dust jackets. Whatever
made us think we could change the world?
Us and our clever punct-
uation marks. A machine gun now, that
would be different. No more unct-
uous adjectives. Cut straight to the verb.
Ars longa, mors brevissima. The life
of poetry breeds the lust
for action, of the most ordinary
sort. Whacking the heads off dandelions,
or bats or bureaucrats,
smashing car windows. Though

at least we've been tolerated,
or even celebrated – which meant
a brief caper in the transient glare
of the sawdust limelight
and your face used later for fishwrap –
but most of the time ignored,
by this crowd that has finally admitted
to itself it doesn't give
too much of a fart for art,
and would rather see a good evisceration
any day. You might as well have been
a dentist, as your father hoped. You

want attention, still? Take your clothes off
at a rush-hour stoplight, howl obscenities,
or shoot someone. You'll get
your name in the paper, maybe,
for what it's worth. In any case

where do we both get off?
Is this small talent we have prized
so much, and rubbed like silver
spoons, until it shone
at least as brightly as neon, really
so much better than the ability
to win the sausage-eating contest,
or juggle six plates at once?
What's the use anyway
of calling the dead back, moving stones,
or making animals cry? I

think of you, loping along at night
to the convenience store, to buy your pint
of milk, your six medium eggs,
your head stuffed full of consonants
like lovely pebbles
you picked up on some lustrous beach
you can't remember – my feather-
headed fool, what have you got
in your almost-empty pockets
that would lure even the lowliest mugger?
Who needs your handful
of glimmering air, your foxfire, your few

underwater crystal tricks
that work only in moonlight?
Noon hits them and they fall apart,
old bones and earth, old teeth, a bundleful
of shadow. Sometimes, I know, the almost-holy
whiteness rooted in our skulls spreads out
like thistles in a vacant lot, a hot powdery
flareup, which is not a halo
and will return
if we're grateful and lucky, and
will end by fusing our neurons. Yet,

singing's a belief
we can't give up.
Anything can become a saint
if you pray to it enough –
spaceship, teacup, wolf –
and what we want is intercession,
that iridescent ribbon
that once held song to object.
We feel everything hovering
on the verge of becoming itself:
the tree is almost a tree, the dog
pissing against it won't be a dog
unless we notice it
and call it by its name: 'Here, dog.'
And so we stand on balconies and rocky
hilltops, and caterwaul our best,
and the world flickers
in and out of being,
and we think it needs our permission. We

shouldn't flatter ourselves: really
it's the other way around. We're at
the mercy of any stray
rabid mongrel or thrown stone or cancerous
ray, or our own
bodies: we were born with mortality's
hook in us, and year by year it drags us
where we're going: down. But

surely there is still
a job to be done by us, at least
time to be passed; for instance, we could
celebrate inner beauty. Gardens.
Love and desire. Lust. Children. Social justice
of various kinds. Include fear and war.
Describe what it is to be tired. Now
we're getting there. But this is much
too pessimistic! Hey, we've got
each other, and a roof, and regular
breakfasts! Cream and mice! For

our sort, elsewhere, it's often worse:
a heaved boot, poisoned meat, or dragged
by the wings or tail off to some wall
or trench and forced to kneel
and have your brains blown out, splattering all over
that Nature we folks are so keen on –
in the company of a million others,
let it be said –
and in the name of what? What noun?
What god or state? The world becomes
one huge deep vowel of horror,
while behind those mildewed flags, the slogans
that always rhyme with *dead*
sit a few old guys making money. So

honestly. Who wants to hear it?
Last time I did that number, honey,
the audience was squirrels.
But I don't need to tell you.
The worst is, now we're respectable.
We're in anthologies. We're taught in schools,
with cleaned-up biographies and skewed photos.
We're part of the mug show now.
In ten years, bet you'll be on a stamp,
where anyone at all can lick you. Ah

Owl and Pussycat, Some Years Later

well, my dearest one, our leaky cardboard
gondola has brought us this far,
us and our paper guitar.
No longer semi-immortal, but moulting owl
and arthritic pussycat, we row

out past the last protecting
sandbar, towards the salty
open sea, the triple dogs'-head gate,
and after that, oblivion.
But sing on, sing
on, someone may still be listening
besides me. The fish for instance. And
if not, sing for the song
itself. In any case,
we still have the moon.

Biographical Notes

Kate Atkinson is the author of three novels: *Behind the Scenes at the Museum*, *Human Croquet* and *Emotionally Weird*. 'The Bodies Vest' is part of a collection of stories entitled *Not The End Of The World* which will be published by Doubleday in 2002.

Ramona Herdman has had her work published in *Staple*, *Lexikon*, *Thumbscrew*, *The Rialto*, *Reactions* and various UEA *<text>*s. Pen&inc will publish her first collection in 2002.

Graeme Gibson was a founding member of the Writers' Union of Canada and President of the Canadian Centre of International PEN. His most recent novel, *Gentleman Death*, is available in McLelland & Stewart's Emblem Editions (2002). Gibson lives in Toronto.

Helle Helle was born in 1965 as Helle Krogh Hansen (she later changed her surname to that of her great grandmother). She attended the Writers' School in Copenhagen in 1989-91, and made her debut in 1993 with *Eksempler på liv* (*Examples of Life*), a collection of short, stylized prose pieces. Since then she has published three short story collections and a novel. She is one of the foremost of a contemporary group of short prose writers in Scandinavia, and is seen by some as an inheritor of the American short story tradition established by Ernest Hemingway and Raymond Carver.

Peter Holm-Jensen holds an MA in Literary Translation from

UEA, works as a Danish-English translator, and is currently translating, among other things, Lars von Trier's film diary *Idioterne (The Idiots)* for Pen&inc.

Jackie Kay is a novelist and short story writer, whose first collection of short fiction, *Why Don't you Stop Talking*, is published by Picador (2002).

Kasia Boddy teaches in the English Department of University College London. She has published interviews and articles on many aspects of contemporary fiction, and is currently completing a book on the representation of boxing in twentieth-century American culture.

Stella Duffy has written three novels: *Singling Out The Couples*, *Eating Cake* and *Immaculate Conceit*, all published by Sceptre. She has also written four crime novels: *Calendar Girl*, *Wavewalker*, *Beneath The Blonde* and *Fresh Flesh*, published by Serpent's Tail. With Lauren Henderson, she is co-editor of the anthology *Tart Noir*.

D.J. Taylor's novels include *English Settlement* (Chatto & Windus, 1996), *Trespass* (Duckworth, 1998) and *The Comedy Man* (Duckworth, 2001). His biography of Thackeray was published in 1999 (Chatto & Windus) and he is currently working on a centenary life of George Orwell.

Rachel Bradford gained a degree in English Literature from UEA. Her short fiction has been published in Pen&inc's *<text>* series and *Pretext* Volume 3.

Nell Dunn's best known work are the novels *Up The Junction* (1963) and *Poor Cow* (1966); and the play *Steaming* (1981). 'Penny and Marilyn' is an extract from her new play *Cancer Tales, True Stories*, which is being produced as part of a King's College symposium 'The Art of Dying'.

Sarah Wood is a screenwriter and film-maker.

Donald Paterson is currently completing a novel, provisionally called *Fire*.

Frances Gapper has written a children's book, a novel, *Saints and Adventurers* (The Women's Press, 1988) and a gardens guide. Her short stories have appeared in magazines and anthologies including *The Penguin Book of Lesbian Short Stories*. Her new short story collection, *Absent Kisses*, will be published by Diva Books in the summer of 2002.

Louise Tondeur won the Curtis Brown Bursary whilst studying at UEA for the MA in Creative Writing. Her first novel *The Water's Edge* will be published by Headline Review in March 2003.

Will Stone is a poet and translator. He holds an MA in Literary Translation from UEA. His translation of *Les Chimeres* by Gerard de Nerval was published by the Menard Press in 1999. His translations of Trakl, Nerval, Baudelaire, Fritsch and Schiele have appeared in the journals *Modern Poetry in Translation*, *Exchanges* and *The International Review*. His essay on poet singer-songwriter Nick Drake was published by Ambros Press in 1998. *Shadow Symposium*, a new collection of poems is forthcoming.

Anthony Vivis is a freelance writer and translator, whose work has appeared at many theatres including the RSC, the Royal Court and the Almeida. His published translations have included the poetry of Rose Auslaender, Gerard de Nerval and Egon Schiele. Since 1998 he has been Chair of East Anglian Writers, and he is currently the Royal Literary Fund Writing Fellow at UEA.

Stephen Chamberlain lives in East London and writes headlines for *The Guardian*.

Graham Mort lives in North Yorkshire where he works as a freelance writer and teaches at Lancaster University. His latest book of poems, *Circular Breathing* (Dangaroo Press, 1996), is a Poetry Book Society recommendation. He is currently project leader for the British Council *Crossing Borders* mentoring scheme for African writers.

Sidura Ludwig is a Canadian writer and journalist currently living in Birmingham, England. She has worked for Canadian Broadcasting Corporation radio, as well as a number of Canadian periodicals. She has published both fiction and non-fiction.

Margaret Atwood is the author of more than twenty-five volumes of poetry, fiction, and nonfiction and is perhaps best known for her novels, which include *The Edible Woman* (1970), *The Handmaid's Tale* (1983), *The Robber Bride* (1994), *Alias Grace* (1996). Her latest novel, *The Blind Assassin*, which won the prestigious Booker Prize, was published in 2000. Atwood's work has been published in more than thirty languages, including Japanese, Turkish, Finnish, Korean, Icelandic and Estonian.

pen&inc

Stop Press!

News from Pen&inc:

Pretext Volume 6 will be guest edited by D.J. Taylor, novelist, biographer and critic.

Volume 6 will be published in October 2002. To submit your work for publication please send an SAE for return of your material to Pretext Editors c/o Pen&inc, EAS, UEA, Norwich, NR4 7TJ.

With ***Reactions 3*** coming out in October 2002, we are calling for submissions for Volume 4. Submissions are invited from writers who have had a first collection or pamphlet published (but not a second), and from those who have not yet reached that stage.

Is your poetry acid or alkaline? As long as it isn't neutral, we'd like to hear from you . . .

If you are interested in submitting work, please send five poems with an SAE to Esther Morgan at the School of English and American Studies, University of East Anglia, Norwich NR4 7TJ.

The poems you send:

- can be on any subject, in any style and of any length.
- should be written in English, but can be in translation.
- should be typed, with your name and address appearing clearly on each.
- must be your own original work.
- must not already be accepted for publication by any magazine (although poems which are due to appear in a first collection or anthology will be considered).
- should be accompanied by a covering letter which lists the titles of your poems, plus a short biography (of no more than 70 words).
- need to reach me no later than 31 March 2003.
- must be good.

The fourth edition of *Reactions* will appear in 2003. *Reactions* is a forum for new poetry by new poets.

Backlist

Pretext

Volume One: *Salvage* £7.99
Pagan Kennedy, Maureen Duffy, David Almond

Volume Two: *Experience* £7.99
Martin Amis, Lorna Sage, Andrew McGahan

Volume Three: *Rancour* £7.99
Tim Parks, Dave Haslam, Amy Prior

Volume Four: *Havoc* £7.99
Lars von Trier, Sarah May, John Burnside

Reactions

Volume One £7.99
Polly Clark, Owen Sheers, Helen Oswald

Volume Two £7.99
Andrew Waterhouse, Helen Ivory, Sibyl Ruth

All prices include p&p

For further information or to order titles please contact:

Pen&inc
English & American Studies
University of East Anglia
Norwich
NR4 7TJ

Please make all cheques payable to: ***University of East Anglia***

www.penandinc.co.uk

e: info@penandinc.co.uk | t: +44 (0)1603 592783 | f: +44 (0)1603 507728